The Big Book of Knit Stitches

Cables, Lace, Ribs, Textures, and a Whole Lot More

From the Editors of Martingale

Martingale®
Create with Confidence

The Big Book of Knit Stitches:
Cables, Lace, Ribs, Textures, and a Whole Lot More
© 2016 by Martingale & Company®

Martingale®
19021 120th Ave. NE, Ste. 102
Bothell, WA 98011-9511 USA
ShopMartingale.com

Printed in China
21 20 19 18 17 16   8 7 6 5 4 3 2 1

Library of Congress Cataloging-in-Publication Data
is available upon request.

ISBN: 978-1-60468-860-3

MISSION STATEMENT

We empower makers who use fabric and yarn
to make life more enjoyable.

CREDITS

PUBLISHER AND
CHIEF VISIONARY OFFICER
Jennifer Erbe Keltner

CONTENT DIRECTOR
Karen Costello Soltys

DESIGN MANAGER
Adrienne Smitke

MANAGING EDITOR
Tina Cook

COVER AND
INTERIOR DESIGNER
Regina Girard

ACQUISITIONS EDITOR
Karen M. Burns

PHOTOGRAPHER
Brent Kane

Contents

Introduction
4

Introduction

When it comes to knitting, many of us are most comfortable following a published pattern, whether it's from a book or magazine, an online download, or our favorite knit shop. But sometimes, you like the shape of a knitted T, but wish it weren't worked in plain Stockinette stitch. Or maybe you like a particular mitten pattern for its shape, but would love to add some sort of a cable design to make it more interesting. Perhaps you'd even like to design your own scarf or afghan from scratch, but you just aren't sure where to start.

That's where *The Big Book of Knit Stitches* comes in. This book doesn't have a single pattern for a knitted garment or accessory. But what it *does* have is 366 stitch patterns that you can use to design your own project or to enhance or change up an existing pattern. That's a lot of design options!

The stitches are organized by type—including lace, cables, bobbles, slip stitches, and more—to make it easy to find the kind of stitch you'd like to work with. Each one lists a stitch repeat, such as "multiple of 10 + 1," which means that you could use this pattern to cover 11, 21, 31, or 41 stitches (or any other multiple of 10, plus 1 more stitch).

What you *won't* find in this book is any reference to gauge. That's because you can use these stitches with any type and weight of yarn you'd like. Simply knit a swatch using your desired yarn to see how it looks. Knit multiple swatches and pick your favorites. Then you can incorporate those stitches into projects from simple scarves to hats, sweaters, afghans, and more. I bet the hardest part will be choosing which stitch to use first!

Karen Costello Soltys
Content Director

Cables, Crosses & Twists

Wave Cable

Worked over 6 sts on a background of reverse St st

Row 1 (RS): Knit.

Row 2: Purl.

Row 3: Cable 6 back.

Row 4: Purl.

Rows 5–8: Rep rows 1 and 2 twice.

Row 9: Cable 6 front.

Row 10: Purl.

Rows 11 and 12: Rep rows 1 and 2.

Rep rows 1–12 for patt.

Giant Cable

Worked over 12 sts on a background of reverse St st

Row 1 (RS): Knit.

Row 2: Purl.

Rows 3 and 4: Rep rows 1 and 2.

Row 5: Cable 12 back.

Row 6: Purl.

Rows 7 and 8: Rep rows 1 and 2.

Rep rows 1–8 for patt.

These instructions result in a cable that twists to the right (shown at right in photo). To twist the cable to the left (shown at left in photo), hold the cable to the front instead of the back in row 5.

Four-Stitch Cable 1

Worked on a background of reverse St st

Row 1 (RS): Knit.

Row 2: Purl.

Rows 3 and 4: Rep rows 1 and 2.

Row 5: Cable 4 back.

Row 6: Purl.

Rep rows 1–6 for patt.

These instructions result in a cable that twists to the right (shown at right in photo). To twist the cable to the left (shown at left in photo), hold the cable to the front instead of the back in row 5.

Six-Stitch Cable

Worked on a background of reverse St st

Row 1 (RS): Knit.

Row 2: Purl.

Row 3: Cable 6 back.

Row 4: Purl.

Rep rows 1–4 for patt.

These instructions result in a cable that twists to the right (shown at right in photo). To twist the cable to the left (shown at left in photo), hold the cable to the front instead of the back in row 3.

Eight-Stitch Cable

Row 1 (RS): Knit.

Row 2: Purl.

Rows 3 and 4: Rep rows 1 and 2.

Row 5: Cable 8 back.

Row 6: Purl.

Rows 7–10: Rep rows 1 and 2 twice.

Rep rows 1–10 for patt.

These instructions result in a cable that twists to the right (shown at right in photo). To twist the cable to the left (shown at left in photo), hold the cable to the front instead of the back in row 5.

Lace and Cables

Multiple of 11 + 7

Row 1 (RS): K1, *YO, sl 1, K1, psso, K1, K2tog, YO, K6; rep from * to last 6 sts, YO, sl 1, K1, psso, K1, K2tog, YO, K1.

Row 2 and all even rows: Purl.

Row 3: K2, *YO, sl 1, K2tog, psso, YO, K8; rep from * to last 5 sts, YO, sl 1, K2tog, psso, YO, K2.

Row 5: Rep row 1.

Row 7: K2, *YO, sl 1, K2tog, psso, YO, K1, cable 6 back, K1; rep from * to last 5 sts, YO, sl 1, K2tog, psso, YO, K2.

Row 8: Purl.

Rep rows 1–8 for patt.

Tight Braid Cable

Worked over 10 sts on a background of reverse St st

Row 1: Purl.

Row 2 (RS): K2, (cable 4 front) twice.

Row 3: Purl.

Row 4: (Cable 4 back) twice, K2.

Rep rows 1–4 for patt.

Mock Wavy Cable Rib

Multiple of 4 + 2

Row 1 (RS): P2, *K2, P2; rep from * to end.

Row 2 and all even rows: K2, *P2, K2; rep from * to end.

Row 3: P2, *cross 2 back, P2; rep from * to end.

Row 5: Rep row 1.

Row 7: P2, *K2tog but do not slip off needle, then insert right-hand needle between these 2 sts and knit first st again, slipping both sts off needle tog, P2; rep from * to end.

Row 8: Rep row 2.

Rep rows 1–8 for patt.

Mock-Cable Rib

Multiple of 7 + 2

Row 1 (RS): P2, *cross 2 back, K3, P2; rep from * to end.

Row 2: K2, *P5, K2; rep from * to end.

Row 3: P2, *K1, cross 2 back, K2, P2; rep from * to end.

Row 4: Rep row 2.

Row 5: P2, *K2, cross 2 back, K1, P2; rep from * to end.

Row 6: Rep row 2.

Row 7: P2, *K3, cross 2 back, P2; rep from * to end.

Row 8: K2, *P5, K2; rep from * to end.

Rep rows 1–8 for patt.

Twisted Basket Weave

Multiple of 8 + 5

Row 1 (RS): P5, *cross 3, P5; rep from * to end.

Row 2: K5, *P3, K5; rep from * to end.

Rows 3 and 4: Rep rows 1 and 2.

Row 5: P1, *cross 3, P5; rep from * to last 4 sts, cross 3, P1.

Row 6: K1, *P3, K5; rep from * to last 4 sts, P3, K1.

Rows 7 and 8: Rep rows 5 and 6.

Rep rows 1–8 for patt.

Cable Fabric

Multiple of 6

Row 1 (RS): Knit.

Row 2 and all even rows: Purl.

Row 3: *K2, cable 4 back; rep from * to end.

Row 5: Knit.

Row 7: *Cable 4 front, K2; rep from * to end.

Row 8: Purl.

Rep rows 1–8 for patt.

Claw Pattern 1

Worked over 8 sts on a background of reverse St st

Upward Claw (shown at left in photo)

Row 1 (RS): Knit.

Row 2: Purl.

Row 3: Cable 4 back, cable 4 front.

Row 4: Purl.

Rep rows 1–4 for patt.

Downward Claw (shown at right in photo)

Row 1 (RS): Knit.

Row 2: Purl.

Row 3: Cable 4 front, cable 4 back.

Row 4: Purl.

Rep rows 1–4 for patt.

 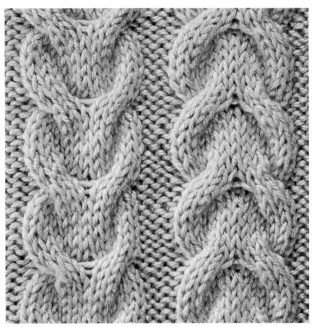

Claw Pattern 2

Worked over 9 sts on a background of reverse St st

Upward Claw (shown at left in photo)

Row 1 (RS): Knit.

Row 2: Purl.

Row 3: Cross 4 right, K1, cross 4 left.

Row 4: Purl.

Rep rows 1–4 for patt.

Downward Claw (shown at right in photo)

Row 1 (RS): Knit.

Row 2: Purl.

Row 3: Cross 4 left, K1, cross 4 right.

Row 4: Purl.

Rep rows 1–4 for patt.

Double Cable

Worked over 12 sts on a background of reverse St st

Upward Cable (shown at left in photo)

Row 1 (RS): Knit.

Row 2: Purl.

Row 3: Cable 6 back, cable 6 front.

Row 4: Purl.

Rows 5–8: Rep rows 1 and 2 twice.

Rep rows 1–8 for patt.

Downward Cable (shown at right in photo)

Row 1 (RS): Knit.

Row 2: Purl.

Row 3: Cable 6 front, cable 6 back.

Row 4: Purl.

Rows 5–8: Rep rows 1 and 2 twice.

Rep rows 1–8 for patt.

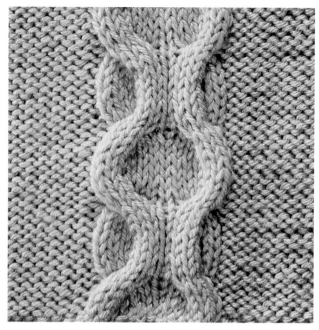

Branched Cable 1

Worked over 10 sts on a background of reverse St st

Row 1 (RS): P3, cable 4 back, P3.

Row 2: K3, P4, K3.

Row 3: P2, twist 3 back, twist 3 front, P2.

Row 4: (K2, P2) twice, K2.

Row 5: P1, twist 3 back, P2, twist 3 front, P1.

Row 6: K1, P2, K4, P2, K1.

Row 7: Twist 3 back, P4, twist 3 front.

Row 8: P2, K6, P2.

Rep rows 1–8 for patt.

Medallion Cable

Worked over 13 sts on a background of reverse St st

Row 1 (RS): Knit.

Row 2: Purl.

Rows 3 and 4: Rep rows 1 and 2.

Row 5: Cable 6 front, K1, cable 6 back.

Row 6: Purl.

Row 7: Knit.

Rows 8–11: Rep rows 6 and 7 twice.

Row 12: Purl.

Row 13: Cable 6 back, K1, cable 6 front.

Row 14: Purl.

Row 15: Knit.

Row 16: Purl.

Rep rows 1–16 for patt.

Staghorn Cable 1

Worked over 16 sts on a background of reverse St st

Row 1 (RS): K4, cable 4 back, cable 4 front, K4.

Row 2: Purl.

Row 3: K2, cable 4 back, K4, cable 4 front, K2.

Row 4: Purl.

Row 5: Cable 4 back, K8, cable 4 front.

Row 6: Purl.

Rep rows 1–6 for patt.

Staghorn Cable 2

Worked over 16 sts on a background of reverse St st

Row 1 (RS): Cable 4 front, K8, cable 4 back.

Row 2: Purl.

Row 3: K2, cable 4 front, K4, cable 4 back, K2.

Row 4: Purl.

Row 5: K4, cable 4 front, cable 4 back, K4.

Row 6: Purl.

Rep rows 1–6 for patt.

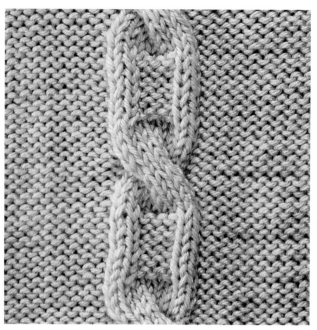

Twist Motif

Multiple of 16 + 2

Rows 1–4: Work in St st, starting with knit row.

Row 5 (RS): K7, cross 2 front, cross 2 back, *K12, cross 2 front, cross 2 back; rep from * to last 7 sts, K7.

Row 6: Purl.

Row 7: K7, cross 2 back, cross 2 front, *K12, cross 2 back, cross 2 front; rep from * to last 7 sts, K7.

Rows 8–14: Work in St st, starting with purl row.

Row 15: K1, *cross 2 back, K12, cross 2 front; rep from * to last st, K1.

Row 16: Purl.

Row 17: K1, *cross 2 front, K12, cross 2 back; rep from * to last st, K1.

Rows 18–20: Work in St st, starting with purl row.

Rep rows 1–20 for patt.

Cable and Box Panel

Worked over 8 sts on a background of reverse St st

Row 1 (RS): Knit.

Row 2: Purl.

Row 3: Cable 8 front.

Rows 4–7: Work in St st, starting with purl row.

Row 8: P2, K4, P2.

Row 9: K2, P4, K2.

Rows 10–13: Rep rows 8 and 9 twice.

Rows 14–16: Work in St st, starting with purl row.

Rep rows 1–16 for patt.

Squares and Twists

Multiple of 10 + 4

Row 1: P4, *K2, P2, K2, P4; rep from * to end.

Row 2 (RS): K4, *P2, cross 2 front, P2, K4; rep from * to end.

Rows 3 and 4: Rep rows 1 and 2.

Row 5: K1, P2, *K2, P4, K2, P2; rep from * to last st, K1.

Row 6: P1, cross 2 front, *P2, K4, P2, cross 2 front; rep from * to last st, P1.

Rows 7 and 8: Rep rows 5 and 6.

Rep rows 1–8 for patt.

Eyelet Mock-Cable Rib

Multiple of 5 + 2

Row 1 (RS): P2, *sl 1, K2, psso, P2; rep from * to end.

Row 2: K2, *P1, YO, P1, K2; rep from * to end.

Row 3: P2, *K3, P2; rep from * to end.

Row 4: K2, *P3, K2; rep from * to end.

Rep rows 1–4 for patt.

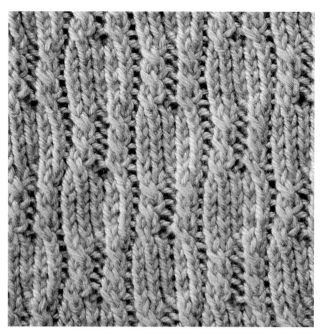

Twisted-Cable Rib

Multiple of 4 + 2

Row 1 (RS): P2, *K2, P2; rep from * to end.

Row 2: K2, *P2, K2; rep from * to end.

Row 3: P2, *K2tog but do not slip off needle, then insert right-hand needle between these 2 sts and knit the first st again, slipping both sts off needle tog, P2; rep from * to end.

Row 4: Rep row 2.

Rep rows 1–4 for patt.

Small Cable Check

Multiple of 12 + 7

Row 1 (RS): *P1, K next 5 sts through back loop, (P1, cross 2 front) twice; rep from * to last 7 sts, P1, K next 5 sts through back loop, P1.

Row 2: *K1, P next 5 sts through back loop, (K1, P2) twice; rep from * to last 7 sts, K1, P next 5 sts through back loop, K1.

Rows 3–6: Rep rows 1 and 2 twice.

Row 7: *(P1, cross 2 front) twice, P1, K next 5 sts through back loop; rep from * to last 7 sts, (P1, cross 2 front) twice, P1.

Row 8: *(K1, P2) twice, K1, P next 5 sts through back loop; rep from * to last 7 sts, (K1, P2) twice, K1.

Rows 9–12: Rep rows 7 and 8 twice.

Rep rows 1–12 for patt.

Mock Cable: Right

Multiple of 4 + 2

Row 1 (RS): P2, *K2, P2; rep from * to end.

Row 2: K2, *P2, K2; rep from * to end.

Row 3: P2, *cross 2 front, P2; rep from * to end.

Row 4: Rep row 2.

Rep rows 1–4 for patt.

Mock Cable: Left

Multiple of 4 + 2

Row 1 (RS): P2, *K2, P2; rep from * to end.

Row 2: K2, *P2, K2; rep from * to end.

Row 3: P2, *cross 2 back, P2; rep from * to end.

Row 4: Rep row 2.

Rep rows 1–4 for patt.

Twist Cable and Ladder Lace

Multiple of 7 + 6

Row 1 (RS): K1, *K2tog, YO twice, sl 1, K1, psso, K3; rep from * to last 5 sts, K2tog, YO twice, sl 1, K1, psso, K1.

Row 2: K2, *(K1, K1 through back loop) into double YO of previous row, K1, P3, K1; rep from * to last 4 sts, (K1, K1 through back loop) into double YO of previous row, K2.

Row 3: K1, *K2tog, YO twice, sl 1, K1, psso, knit into third st on left-hand needle, then knit into second st, then knit into first st, slipping all 3 sts onto right-hand needle tog; rep from * to last 5 sts, K2tog, YO twice, sl 1, K1, psso, K1.

Row 4: Rep row 2.

Rep rows 1–4 for patt.

Honeycomb Cable

Worked over 12 sts on a background of reverse St st

Row 1 (RS): K4, cross 2 front, cross 2 back, K4.

Row 2 and all even rows: Purl.

Row 3: K2, (cross 2 front, cross 2 back) twice, K2.

Row 5: (Cross 2 front, cross 2 back) 3 times.

Row 7: (Cross 2 back, cross 2 front) 3 times.

Row 9: K2, (cross 2 back, cross 2 front) twice, K2.

Row 11: K4, cross 2 back, cross 2 front, K4.

Row 12: Purl.

Rep rows 1–12 for patt.

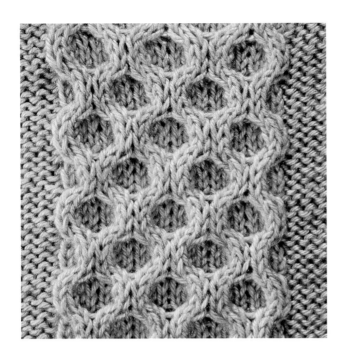

Honeycomb Pattern

Worked over a multiple of 8 sts on a background of reverse St st. The example shown is worked over 24 sts.

Row 1 (RS): *Cable 4 back, cable 4 front; rep from * to end of panel.

Row 2 and all even rows: Purl.

Row 3: Knit.

Row 5: *Cable 4 front, cable 4 back; rep from * to end of panel.

Row 7: Knit.

Row 8: Purl.

Rep rows 1–8 for patt.

Garter and Stockinette Cable

Worked over 8 sts on a background of reverse St st

Row 1 (RS): Knit.

Row 2: P4, K4.

Rows 3–6: Rep rows 1 and 2 twice.

Row 7: Cable 8 back.

Row 8: K4, P4.

Row 9: Knit.

Rows 10–18: Rep rows 8 and 9 four more times; then rep row 8 once more.

Row 19: Cable 8 back.

Row 20: Rep row 2.

Row 21: Knit.

Rows 22–24: Rep rows 20 and 21; then rep row 20 once more.

Rep rows 1–24 for patt.

Cable Circles

Worked over 12 sts on a background of reverse St st

Row 1 (RS): Purl.

Row 2: Knit.

Row 3: P3, K6, P3.

Row 4: K3, P6, K3.

Row 5: Cable 6 back, cable 6 front.

Rows 6–10: Work in St st, starting with purl row.

Row 11: Twist 6 front, twist 6 back.

Row 12: Rep row 4.

Rep rows 1–12 for patt.

Knotted Cable

Worked over 6 sts on a background of reverse St st

Row 1 (RS): K2, P2, K2.

Row 2 and all even rows: P2, K2, P2.

Row 3: Cross 6.

Rows 5, 7, and 9: Rep row 1.

Row 10: Rep row 2.

Rep rows 1–10 for patt.

Little Cable Stitch

Multiple of 6 + 2

Row 1 (RS): Knit.

Row 2: Purl.

Row 3: P2, *cross 2 back, cross 2 front, P2; rep from * to end.

Row 4: Purl.

Row 5: Knit.

Row 6: Purl.

Rep rows 1–6 for patt.

Woven Cable Stitch

Multiple of 4

Row 1 (RS): *Cable 4 front; rep from * to end.

Row 2: Purl.

Row 3: K2, *cable 4 back; rep from * to last 2 sts, K2.

Row 4: Purl.

Rep rows 1–4 for patt.

Nine-Stitch Braid

Done on a background of reverse St st

Upward Braid (shown at left in photo)

Row 1 (RS): Knit.

Row 2 and all even rows: Purl.

Row 3: Cable 6 back, K3.

Row 5: Knit.

Row 7: K3, cable 6 front.

Row 8: Purl.

Rep rows 1–8 for patt.

Downward Braid (shown at right in photo)

Row 1 (RS): Knit.

Row 2 and all even rows: Purl.

Row 3: Cable 6 front, K3.

Row 5: Knit.

Row 7: K3, cable 6 back.

Row 8: Purl.

Rep rows 1–8 for patt.

Six-Stitch Braid

Done on a background of reverse St st

Upward Braid (shown at left in photo)

Row 1 (RS): Cable 4 back, K2.

Row 2: Purl.

Row 3: K2, cable 4 front.

Row 4: Purl.

Rep rows 1–4 for patt.

Downward Braid (shown at right in photo)

Row 1 (RS): Cable 4 front, K2.

Row 2: Purl.

Row 3: K2, cable 4 back.

Row 4: Purl.

Rep rows 1–4 for patt.

Four-Stitch Cable 2

Worked on a background of reverse St st

Row 1 (RS): Knit.

Row 2: Purl.

Row 3: Cable 4 back.

Row 4: Purl.

Rep rows 1–4 for patt.

These instructions result in a cable that twists to the right (shown at right in photo). To twist the cable to the left (shown at left in photo), hold the cable to the front instead of the back in row 3.

Woven Lattice Pattern

Multiple of 6 + 2

Row 1: K3, P4, *K2, P4; rep from * to last st, K1.

Row 2 (RS): P1, cable 4 front, *P2, cable 4 front; rep from * to last 3 sts, P3.

Row 3: Rep row 1.

Row 4: P3, *K2, twist 4 back; rep from * to last 5 sts, K4, P1.

Row 5: K1, P4, *K2, P4; rep from * to last 3 sts, K3.

Row 6: P3, cable 4 back, *P2, cable 4 back; rep from * to last st, P1.

Row 7: Rep row 5.

Row 8: P1, K4, *twist 4 front, K2; rep from * to last 3 sts, P3.

Rep rows 1–8 for patt.

Allover Lattice Stitch

Multiple of 12 + 2

Row 1: Purl.

Row 2 (RS): Knit.

Row 3: Purl.

Row 4: K1, *cable 4 back, K4, cable 4 front; rep from * to last st, K1.

Rows 5–7: Work in St st, starting with purl row.

Row 8: K3, cable 4 front, cable 4 back, *K4, cable 4 front, cable 4 back; rep from * to last 3 sts, K3.

Rep rows 1–8 for patt.

Woven Cables in Relief

Multiple of 15 + 2

Row 1 (RS): Knit.

Row 2: Purl.

Row 3: K1, cable 10 front, *K5, cable 10 front; rep from * to last 6 sts, K6.

Rows 4–8: Work in St st, starting with purl row.

Row 9: K6, cable 10 back, *K5, cable 10 back; rep from * to last st, K1.

Rows 10–12: Work in St st, starting with purl row.

Rep rows 1–12 for patt.

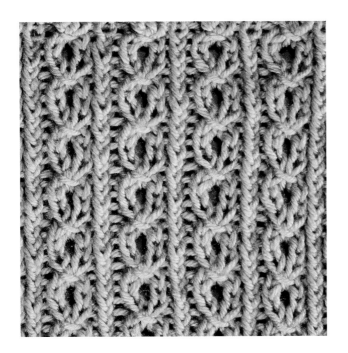

Open Twisted Rib

Multiple of 5 + 3

Row 1: K1, P1 through back loop, K1, *P2, K1, P1 through back loop, K1; rep from * to end.

Row 2 (RS): P1, K1 through back loop, P1, *K1, YO, K1, P1, K1 through back loop, P1; rep from * to end.

Row 3: K1, P1 through back loop, K1, *P3, K1, P1 through back loop, K1; rep from * to end.

Row 4: P1, K1 through back loop, P1, *K3, pass third st on right-hand needle over first 2 sts, P1, K1 through back loop, P1; rep from * to end.

Rep rows 1–4 for patt.

Branched Cable 2

Worked over 10 sts on a background of reverse St st

Row 1 (RS): P3, cable 4 front, P3.

Row 2: K3, P4, K3.

Row 3: P2, cross 3 back, cross 3 front, P2.

Row 4: K2, P6, K2.

Row 5: P1, cross 3 back, K2, cross 3 front, P1.

Row 6: K1, P8, K1.

Row 7: Cross 3 back, K4, cross 3 front.

Row 8: Purl.

Rep rows 1–8 for patt.

Eyelet Cable

Multiple of 8 + 1

Row 1 (RS): P1, *cross 3 together, P1, K3, P1; rep from * to end.

Row 2: K1, *P3, K1, P1, YO, P1, K1; rep from * to end.

Row 3: P1, *K3, P1, cross 3 together, P1; rep from * to end.

Row 4: K1, *P1, YO, P1, K1, P3, K1; rep from * to end.

Rep rows 1–4 for patt.

Six-Stitch Spiral Cable

Done on a background of reverse St st

Row 1 (RS): Cross 2 front 3 times.

Row 2: Purl.

Row 3: K1, cross 2 front twice, K1.

Row 4: Purl.

Rep rows 1–4 for patt.

Little Pearl Cable

Worked over 4 sts on a background of reverse St st

Row 1 (RS): Cross 2 front, cross 2 back.

Row 2: Purl.

Row 3: Cross 2 back, cross 2 front.

Row 4: Purl.

Rep rows 1–4 for patt.

Braided Cable

Worked over 9 sts on a background of reverse St st

Row 1: Twist 3 front, twist 3 back, twist 3 front.

Row 2: P2, K2, P4, K1.

Row 3: P1, cable 4 back, P2, K2.

Row 4: Rep row 2.

Row 5: Twist 3 back, twist 3 front, twist 3 back.

Row 6: K1, P4, K2, P2.

Row 7: K2, P2, cable 4 front, P1.

Row 8: Rep row 6.

Rep rows 1–8 for patt.

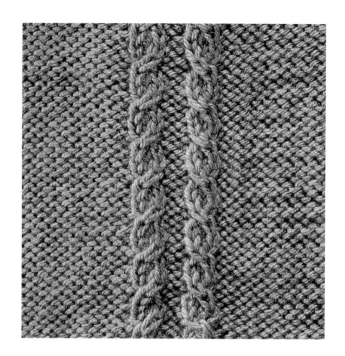

Slipped Three-Stitch Cable

Done on a background of reverse St st

Slipped to the Right (shown at left in photo)

Row 1 (RS): K2, sl 1.

Row 2: Sl 1, P2.

Row 3: Cable 3 right.

Row 4: Purl.

Rep rows 1–4 for patt.

Slipped to the Left (shown at right in photo)

Row 1 (RS): Sl 1, K2.

Row 2: P2, sl 1.

Row 3: Cable 3 left.

Row 4: Purl.

Rep rows 1–4 for patt.

Forked Cable

Multiple of 8 + 2

Row 1: Purl.

Row 2 (RS): P3, K4, *P4, K4; rep from * to last 3 sts, P3.

Rows 3–7: Rep rows 1 and 2 twice, then rep row 1 once more.

Row 8: K3, P4, *K4, P4; rep from * to last 3 sts, K3.

Row 9: Purl.

Row 10: K1, *cable 4 front, cable 4 back; rep from * to last st, K1.

Rep rows 1–10 for patt.

Loose Woven Cables

Multiple of 6 + 2

Row 1 (RS): Knit.

Row 2: K1, knit to last st, wrapping yarn twice around needle for each st, K1.

Row 3: K1, *cable 6 back (dropping extra loops); rep from * to last st, K1.

Rows 4 and 5: Knit.

Row 6: K4, *knit to last 4 sts, wrapping yarn twice around needle for each st, K4.

Row 7: K4, *cable 6 front (dropping extra loops); rep from * to last 4 sts, K4.

Row 8: Knit.

Rep rows 1–8 for patt.

Thirteen-Stitch Claw Pattern

Done on a background of reverse St st

Upward Claw (shown at left in photo)

Row 1 (RS): Knit.

Row 2: Purl.

Row 3: Cable 6 back, K1, cable 6 front.

Row 4: Purl.

Rep rows 1–4 for patt.

Downward Claw (shown at right in photo)

Row 1 (RS): Knit.

Row 2: Purl.

Row 3: Cable 6 front, K1, cable 6 back.

Row 4: Purl.

Rep rows 1–4 for patt.

Small Twist Pattern

Multiple of 8 + 6

Row 1 (RS): Knit.

Row 2 and all even rows: Purl.

Row 3: K1, cable 4 front, *K4, cable 4 front; rep from * to last st, K1.

Row 5: Knit.

Row 7: K5, cable 4 front, *K4, cable 4 front; rep from * to last 5 sts, K5.

Row 8: Purl.

Rep rows 1–8 for patt.

Honeycomb Stitch

Multiple of 4

Row 1 (RS): *Cross 2 front, cross 2 back; rep from * to end.

Row 2: Purl.

Row 3: *Cross 2 back, cross 2 front; rep from * to end.

Row 4: Purl.

Rep rows 1–4 for patt.

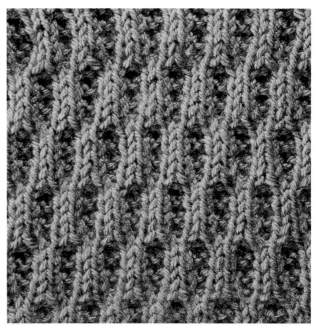

Candle-Flame Stitch

Multiple of 4 + 2

Row 1 (RS): K2, *P2, K2; rep from * to end.

Row 2: P2, *K2, P2; rep from * to end.

Row 3: K2, *P2, cross 2 front; rep from * to last 4 sts, P2, K2.

Rows 4 and 5: Rep row 2.

Row 6: Rep row 1.

Row 7: P2, *cross 2 front, P2; rep from * to end.

Row 8: Rep row 1.

Rep rows 1–8 for patt.

Honeycomb Cable Stitch

Multiple of 4 + 2

Row 1 (RS): Knit.

Row 2: P2, *K2, P2; rep from * to end.

Row 3: Knit.

Row 4: Rep row 2.

Row 5: K1, *cross 2 front, cross 2 back; rep from * to last st, K1.

Row 6: K2, *P2, K2; rep from * to end.

Row 7: Knit.

Row 8: Rep row 6.

Row 9: Knit.

Row 10: Rep row 6.

Row 11: K1, *cross 2 back, cross 2 front; rep from * to last st, K1.

Row 12: Rep row 2.

Rep rows 1–12 for patt.

Lichen Twist

Multiple of 4 + 2

Row 1 (RS): *K1 through back loop; rep from * to end.

Row 2: *P1 through back loop; rep from * to end.

Row 3: P2, *cross 2 back, P2; rep from * to end.

Row 4: K2, *P2, K2; rep from * to end.

Row 5: Rep row 1.

Row 6: Rep row 2.

Row 7: K2, *P2, cross 2 back; rep from * to last 4 sts, P2, K2.

Row 8: P2, *K2, P2; rep from * to end.

Rep rows 1–8 for patt.

Little Cable Fabric

Multiple of 4 + 1

Row 1 (RS): K1, *sl 1, K3; rep from * to end.

Row 2: *P3, sl 1; rep from * to last st, P1.

Row 3: K1, *cable 3 left, K1; rep from * to end.

Row 4: Purl.

Row 5: K5, *sl 1, K3; rep from * to end.

Row 6: *P3, sl 1; rep from * to last 5 sts, P5.

Row 7: K3, *cable 3 right, K1; rep from * to last 2 sts, K2.

Row 8: Purl.

Rep rows 1–8 for patt.

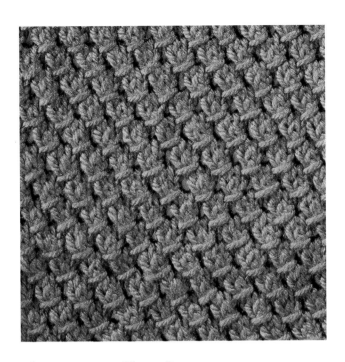

Crocus Buds

Multiple of 2 + 1

Row 1 (RS): K1, *YO, K2; rep from * to end.

Row 2: P1, *P3, pass third st on right-hand needle over first 2 sts; rep from * to end.

Row 3: *K2, YO; rep from * to last st, K1.

Row 4: *P3, pass third st on right-hand needle over first 2 sts; rep from * to last st, P1.

Rep rows 1–4 for patt.

Knotted Openwork

Multiple of 3

Row 1: Purl.

Row 2 (RS): K2, *YO, K3, pass third st on right-hand needle over first 2 sts; rep from * to last st, K1.

Row 3: Purl.

Row 4: K1, *K3, pass third st on right-hand needle over first 2 sts, YO; rep from * to last 2 sts, K2.

Rep rows 1–4 for patt.

Tunnel Lace

Multiple of 3 + 2

Row 1 (RS): P2, *YO, K1, YO, P2; rep from * to end.

Row 2: K2, *P3, K2; rep from * to end.

Row 3: P2, *K3, P2; rep from * to end.

Row 4: K2, *P3tog, K2; rep from * to end.

Rep rows 1–4 for patt.

Waterfall

Multiple of 6 + 3

Row 1 (RS): P3, *K3, YO, P3; rep from * to end.

Row 2: K3, *P4, K3; rep from * to end.

Row 3: P3, *K1, K2tog, YO, K1, P3; rep from * to end.

Row 4: K3, *P2, P2tog, K3; rep from * to end.

Row 5: P3, *K1, YO, K2tog, P3; rep from * to end.

Row 6: K3, *P3, K3; rep from * to end.

Rep rows 1–6 for patt.

Fishtail Lace

Multiple of 8 + 1

Row 1 (RS): K1, *YO, K2, sl 1, K2tog, psso, K2, YO, K1; rep from * to end.

Row 2: Purl.

Row 3: K2, *YO, K1, sl 1, K2tog, psso, K1, YO, K3; rep from * to last 7 sts, YO, K1, sl 1, K2tog, psso, K1, YO, K2.

Row 4: Purl.

Row 5: K3, *YO, sl 1, K2tog, psso, YO, K5; rep from * to last 6 sts, YO, sl 1, K2tog, psso, YO, K3.

Row 6: Purl.

Rep rows 1–6 for patt.

Ridged Lace 1

Multiple of 2 + 1

Rows 1–3: Purl.

Row 4 (RS): K1, *YO, sl 1, K1, psso; rep from * to end.

Rows 5–7: Purl.

Row 8: K1, *YO, K2tog; rep from * to end.

Rep rows 1–8 for patt.

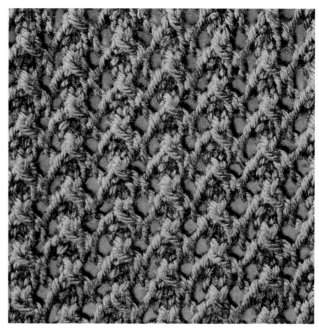

Feather Lace

Multiple of 6 + 1

Row 1 (RS): K1, *YO, K2tog through back loop, K1, K2tog, YO, K1; rep from * to end.

Row 2 and all even rows: Purl.

Row 3: K1, *YO, K1, sl 1, K2tog, psso, K1, YO, K1; rep from * to end.

Row 5: K1, *K2tog, YO, K1, YO, K2tog through back loop, K1; rep from * to end.

Row 7: K2tog, *(K1, YO) twice, K1, sl 1, K2tog, psso; rep from * to last 5 sts, (K1, YO) twice, K1, K2tog through back loop.

Row 8: Purl.

Rep rows 1–8 for patt.

Trellis Lace

Multiple of 6 + 5

Row 1 (RS): K4, *YO, sl 1, K2tog, psso, YO, K3; rep from * to last st, K1.

Row 2: Purl.

Row 3: K1, *YO, sl 1, K2tog, psso, YO, K3; rep from * to last 4 sts, YO, sl 1, K2tog, psso, YO, K1.

Row 4: Purl.

Rep rows 1–4 for patt.

Little Lace Panel

Worked over 5 sts on a background of St st

Row 1 (RS): K1, YO, K3, YO, K1.

Row 2: Purl.

Row 3: K2, sl 1, K2tog, psso, K2.

Row 4: Purl.

Rep rows 1–4 for patt.

Faggoted Panel

Worked over 9 sts on a background of St st

Row 1 (RS): P1, K1, K2tog, YO, K1, YO, K2tog through back loop, K1, P1.

Row 2: K1, P7, K1.

Row 3: P1, K2tog, YO, K3, YO, K2tog through back loop, P1.

Row 4: Rep row 2.

Rep rows 1–4 for patt.

Diamond Panel

Worked over 11 sts on a background of St st

Row 1 (RS): P2, K2tog, (K1, YO) twice, K1, sl 1, K1, psso, P2.

Row 2 and all even rows: K2, P7, K2.

Row 3: P2, K2tog, YO, K3, YO, sl 1, K1, psso, P2.

Row 5: P2, K1, YO, sl 1, K1, psso, K1, K2tog, YO, K1, P2.

Row 7: P2, K2, YO, sl 1, K2tog, psso, YO, K2, P2.

Row 8: Rep row 2.

Rep rows 1–8 for patt.

Leaf Panel

Worked over 24 sts on a background of St st

Row 1 (RS): Sl 1, K2tog, psso, K7, YO, K1, YO, P2, YO, K1, YO, K7, K3tog.

Row 2 and all even rows: P11, K2, P11.

Row 3: Sl 1, K2tog, psso, K6, (YO, K1) twice, P2, (K1, YO) twice, K6, K3tog.

Row 5: Sl 1, K2tog, psso, K5, YO, K1, YO, K2, P2, K2, YO, K1, YO, K5, K3tog.

Row 7: Sl 1, K2tog, psso, K4, YO, K1, YO, K3, P2, K3, YO, K1, YO, K4, K3tog.

Row 9: Sl 1, K2tog, psso, K3, YO, K1, YO, K4, P2, K4, YO, K1, YO, K3, K3tog.

Row 10: Rep row 2.

Rep rows 1–10 for patt.

Wheatear Stitch

Multiple of 8 + 6

Row 1 (RS): P5, *K2, YO, sl 1, K1, psso, P4; rep from * to last st, P1.

Row 2: K5, *P2, YO, P2tog, K4; rep from * to last st, K1.

Rows 3–8: Rep rows 1 and 2 three more times.

Row 9: P1, *K2, YO, sl 1, K1, psso, P4; rep from * to last 5 sts, K2, YO, sl 1, K1, psso, P1.

Row 10: K1, *P2, YO, P2tog, K4; rep from * to last 5 sts, P2, YO, P2tog, K1.

Rows 11–16: Rep rows 9 and 10 three more times.

Rep rows 1–16 for patt.

Flower Buds

Multiple of 8 + 5

Row 1 (RS): K3, *YO, K2, P3tog, K2, YO, K1; rep from * to last 2 sts, K2.

Row 2: Purl.

Rows 3–6: Rep rows 1 and 2 twice more.

Row 7: K2, P2tog, *K2, YO, K1, YO, K2, P3tog; rep from * to last 9 sts, K2, YO, K1, YO, K2, P2tog, K2.

Row 8: Purl.

Rows 9–12: Rep rows 7 and 8 twice more.

Rep rows 1–12 for patt.

Snowdrop Lace

Multiple of 8 + 5

Row 1 (RS): K1, *YO, sl 1, K2tog, psso, YO, K5; rep from * to last 4 sts, YO, sl 1, K2tog, psso, YO, K1.

Row 2 and all even rows: Purl.

Row 3: Rep row 1.

Row 5: K4, *YO, sl 1, K1, psso, K1, K2tog, YO, K3; rep from * to last st, K1.

Row 7: K1, *YO, sl 1, K2tog, psso, YO, K1; rep from * to end.

Row 8: Rep row 2.

Rep rows 1–8 for patt.

Feather Openwork

Multiple of 5 + 2

Row 1 (RS): K1, *K2tog, YO, K1, YO, sl 1, K1, psso; rep from * to last st, K1.

Row 2: Purl.

Rep rows 1 and 2 for patt.

Feather and Fan

Multiple of 18 + 2

Row 1 (RS): Knit.

Row 2: Purl.

Row 3: K1, *K2tog 3 times, (YO, K1) 6 times, K2tog 3 times; rep from * to last st, K1.

Row 4: Knit.

Rep rows 1–4 for patt.

Chevron and Feather

Multiple of 13 + 1

Row 1 (RS): *K1, YO, K4, K2tog, sl 1, K1, psso, K4, YO; rep from * to last st, K1.

Row 2: Purl.

Rep rows 1 and 2 for patt.

Pillar Openwork

Multiple of 3 + 2

Row 1 (RS): K1, *YO, sl 1, K2, psso the K2; rep from * to last st, K1.

Row 2: Purl.

Rep rows 1 and 2 for patt.

Little Fountain Pattern

Multiple of 4 + 1

Row 1 (RS): K1, *YO, K3, YO, K1; rep from * to end.

Row 2: Purl.

Row 3: K2, sl 1, K2tog, psso, *K3, sl 1, K2tog, psso; rep from * to last 2 sts, K2.

Row 4: Purl.

Rep rows 1–4 for patt.

Braided Openwork

Multiple of 2

Row 1: Purl.

Row 2 (RS): K1, *sl 1, K1, psso, M1; rep from * to last st, K1.

Row 3: Purl.

Row 4: K1, *M1, K2tog; rep from * to last st, K1.

Rep rows 1–4 for patt.

Cellular Stitch

Multiple of 4 + 2

Row 1 (RS): K1, YO, sl 1, K2tog, psso, *YO, K1, YO, sl 1, K2tog, psso; rep from * to last 2 sts, YO, K1, YO, K1.

Row 2: Purl.

Row 3: K1, YO, K2tog, *YO, sl 1, K2tog, psso, YO, K1; rep from * to last 4 sts, YO, sl 1, K2tog, psso, K1.

Row 4: Purl.

Rep rows 1–4 for patt.

Oblique Openwork

Multiple of 2

Row 1 (RS): K1, P1, *YO, K1, P1; rep from * to end.

Row 2: *K1, P2tog, YO; rep from * to last 2 sts, K1, P1.

Row 3: K1, P1, *YO, K2tog, P1; rep from * to end.

Rep rows 2 and 3 for patt.

Butterfly Lace

Multiple of 8 + 7

Row 1 (RS): K1, *K2tog, YO, K1, YO, sl 1, K1, psso, K3; rep from * to last 6 sts, K2tog, YO, K1, YO, sl 1, K1, psso, K1.

Row 2: P3, *sl 1, P7; rep from * to last 4 sts, sl 1, P3.

Rows 3 and 4: Rep rows 1 and 2.

Row 5: K5, *K2tog, YO, K1, YO, sl 1, K1, psso, K3; rep from * to last 2 sts, K2.

Row 6: P7, *sl 1, P7; rep from * to end.

Rows 7 and 8: Rep rows 5 and 6.

Rep rows 1–8 for patt.

Garter Drop Stitch

Any number of stitches

Rows 1–4: Work in garter st (knit every row).

Row 5: *K1, winding yarn twice around needle; rep from * to end.

Row 6: Knit to end, dropping the extra loops.

Rep rows 1–6 for patt.

Lattice Lace

Multiple of 7 + 2

Row 1 (RS): K3, *K2tog, YO, K5; rep from * to last 6 sts, K2tog, YO, K4.

Row 2: P2, *P2tog through back loop, YO, P1, YO, P2tog, P2; rep from * to end.

Row 3: K1, *K2tog, YO, K3, YO, sl 1, K1, psso; rep from * to last st, K1.

Row 4: Purl.

Row 5: K1, *YO, sl 1, K1, psso, K5; rep from * to last st, K1.

Row 6: *P1, YO, P2tog, P2, P2tog through back loop, YO; rep from * to last 2 sts, P2.

Row 7: *K3, YO, sl 1, K1, psso, K2tog, YO; rep from * to last 2 sts, K2.

Row 8: Purl.

Rep rows 1–8 for patt.

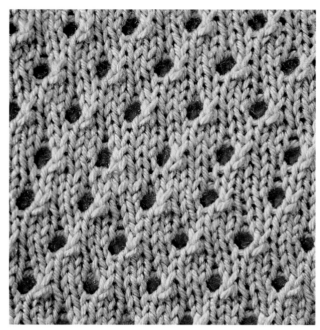

Lacy Checks

Multiple of 6 + 5

Row 1 (RS): K1, *YO, sl 1, K2tog, psso, YO, K3; rep from * to last 4 sts, YO, sl 1, K2tog, psso, YO, K1.

Row 2 and all even rows: Purl.

Row 3: Rep row 1.

Row 5: Knit.

Row 7: K4, *YO, sl 1, K2tog, psso, YO, K3; rep from * to last st, K1.

Row 9: Rep row 7.

Row 11: Knit.

Row 12: Purl.

Rep rows 1–12 for patt.

Staggered Eyelets

Multiple of 4 + 3

Row 1: Knit.

Row 2: Purl.

Row 3 (RS): *K2, K2tog, YO; rep from * to last 3 sts, K3.

Row 4: Purl.

Row 5: Knit.

Row 6: Purl.

Row 7: *K2tog, YO, K2; rep from * to last 3 sts, K2tog, YO, K1.

Row 8: Purl.

Rep rows 1–8 for patt.

Fir Cone

Multiple of 10 + 1

Row 1: Purl.

Row 2 (RS): K1, *YO, K3, sl 1, K2tog, psso, K3, YO, K1; rep from * to end.

Rows 3–8: Rep rows 1 and 2 three more times.

Row 9: Purl.

Row 10: K2tog, *K3, YO, K1, YO, K3, sl 1, K2tog, psso; rep from * to last 9 sts, K3, YO, K1, YO, K3, sl 1, K1, psso.

Rows 11–16: Rep rows 9 and 10 three more times.

Rep rows 1–16 for patt.

Wavy Eyelet Rib

Multiple of 7 + 2

Row 1 (RS): *P2, YO, sl 1, K1, psso, K1, K2tog, YO; rep from * to last 2 sts, P2.

Row 2 and all even rows: K2, *P5, K2; rep from * to end.

Row 3: Rep row 1.

Row 5: Rep row 1.

Row 7: *P2, K5; rep from * to last 2 sts, P2.

Row 9: *P2, K2tog, YO, K1, YO, sl 1, K1, psso; rep from * to last 2 sts, P2.

Row 11: Rep row 9.

Row 13: Rep row 9.

Row 15: Rep row 7.

Row 16: Rep row 2.

Rep rows 1–16 for patt.

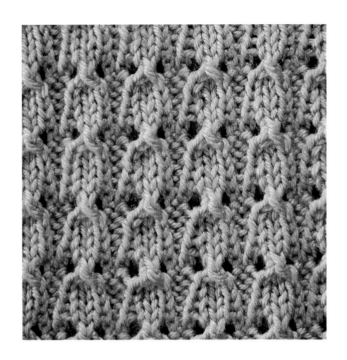

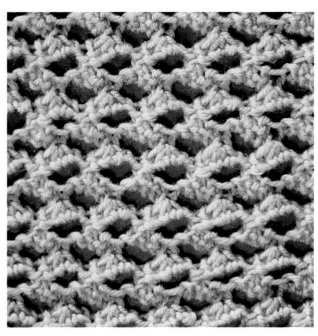

Bluebell Rib

Multiple of 5 + 2

Row 1 (RS): P2, *K3, P2; rep from * to end.

Row 2: K2, *P3, K2; rep from * to end.

Rows 3 and 4: Rep rows 1 and 2.

Row 5: P2, *YO, sl 1, K2tog, psso, YO, P2; rep from * to end.

Row 6: Rep row 2.

Rep rows 1–6 for patt.

Grand Eyelets

Multiple of 4

Row 1: P2, *YO, P4tog; rep from * to last 2 sts, P2.

Row 2: K3, (K1, P1, K1) into next st, *K1, (K1, P1, K1) into next st; rep from * to last 2 sts, K2.

Row 3: Knit.

Rep rows 1–3 for patt.

Vandyke Lace Panel 1

Worked over 17 sts on a background of St st

Row 1 (RS): *K2tog, YO, K1, YO, sl 1, K1, psso,* K3, YO, sl 1, K1, psso, K2; rep from * to * once more.

Row 2: Purl.

Row 3: (K2tog, YO, K1, YO, sl 1, K1, psso, K1) twice, K2tog, YO, K1, YO, sl 1, K1, psso.

Row 4: Purl.

Row 5: *K2tog, YO, K1, YO, sl 1, K1, psso,* K2tog, YO, K3, YO, sl 1, K1, psso; rep from * to * once more.

Row 6: Purl.

Rep rows 1–6 for patt.

Vandyke Lace Panel 2

Worked over 9 sts on a background of St st

Row 1 (RS): K4, YO, sl 1, K1, psso, K3.

Row 2 and all even rows: Purl.

Row 3: K2, K2tog, YO, K1, YO, sl 1, K1, psso, K2.

Row 5: K1, K2tog, YO, K3, YO, sl 1, K1, psso, K1.

Row 7: K2tog, YO, K5, YO, sl 1, K1, psso.

Row 8: Purl.

Rep rows 1–8 for patt.

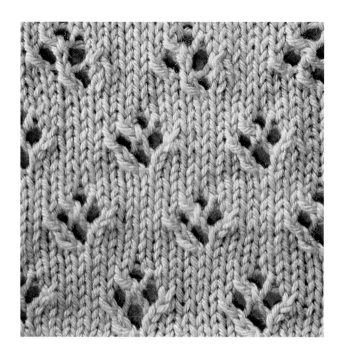

Tulip Lace

Multiple of 8 + 7

Row 1 (RS): Knit.

Row 2 and all even rows: Purl.

Row 3: K3, *YO, sl 1, K1, psso, K6; rep from * to last 4 sts, YO, sl 1, K1, psso, K2.

Row 5: K1, *K2tog, YO, K1, YO, sl 1, K1, psso, K3; rep from * to last 6 sts, K2tog, YO, K1, YO, sl 1, K1, psso, K1.

Row 7: Rep row 3.

Row 9: Knit.

Row 11: K7, *YO, sl 1, K1, psso, K6; rep from * to end.

Row 13: K5, *K2tog, YO, K1, YO, sl 1, K1, psso, K3; rep from * to last 2 sts, K2.

Row 15: Rep row 11.

Row 16: Purl.

Rep rows 1–16 for patt.

Fishtail Lace Panel

Worked over 11 sts on a background of St st

Row 1 (RS): P1, K1, YO, K2, sl 1, K2tog, psso, K2, YO, K1, P1.

Row 2: K1, P9, K1.

Row 3: P1, K2, YO, K1, sl 1, K2tog, psso, K1, YO, K2, P1.

Row 4: Rep row 2.

Row 5: P1, K3, YO, sl 1, K2tog, psso, YO, K3, P1.

Row 6: Rep row 2.

Rep rows 1–6 for patt.

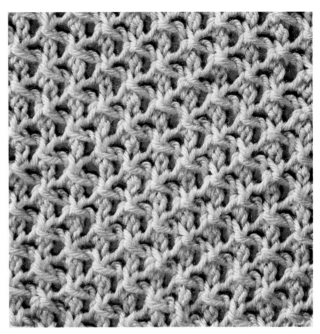

Diagonal Openwork

Multiple of 4 + 2

Row 1 (RS): *K1, YO, sl 1, K2tog, psso, YO; rep from * to last 2 sts, K2.

Row 2 and all even rows: Purl.

Row 3: K2, *YO, sl 1, K2tog, psso, YO, K1; rep from * to end.

Row 5: K2tog, YO, K1, YO, *sl 1, K2tog, psso, YO, K1, YO; rep from * to last 3 sts, sl 1, K1, psso, K1.

Row 7: K1, K2tog, YO, K1, YO, *sl 1, K2tog, psso, YO, K1, YO; rep from * to last 2 sts, sl 1, K1, psso.

Row 8: Purl.

Rep rows 1–8 for patt.

Cell Stitch

Multiple of 4 + 3

Row 1 (RS): K2, *YO, sl 1, K2tog, psso, YO, K1; rep from * to last st, K1.

Row 2: Purl.

Row 3: K1, K2tog, YO, K1, *YO, sl 1, K2tog, psso, YO, K1; rep from * to last 3 sts, YO, sl 1, K1, psso, K1.

Row 4: Purl.

Rep rows 1–4 for patt.

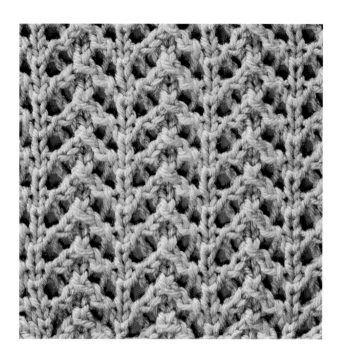

Little Arrowhead

Multiple of 6 + 1

Row 1 (RS): K1, *YO, sl 1, K1, psso, K1, K2tog, YO, K1; rep from * to end.

Row 2: Purl.

Row 3: K2, *YO, sl 1, K2tog, psso, YO, K3; rep from * to last 5 sts, YO, sl 1, K2tog, psso, YO, K2.

Row 4: Purl.

Rep rows 1–4 for patt.

Ridged Openwork

Multiple of 2 + 1

Row 1 (RS): Purl.

Row 2: *P2tog; rep from * to last st, P1.

Row 3: P1, *purl through horizontal strand of yarn lying between stitch just worked and next st, P1; rep from * to end.

Row 4: P1, *YO, P2tog; rep from * to end.

Rep rows 1–4 for patt.

Ridged Eyelet Border

Multiple of 2 + 1

Worked on a background of St st

Rows 1–3: Knit.

Row 4 (WS): *P2tog, YO; rep from * to last st, P1.

Rows 5–7: Knit.

Row 8: Purl.

Rows 9–16: Rep rows 1–8.

Row 17: Knit.

Row 18: Purl.

Row 19: Knit.

Row 20: Purl.

Rep rows 1–20 for patt.

Zigzag Eyelet Panel

Worked over 11 sts on a background of St st

Row 1 (RS): K6, YO, sl 1, K1, psso, K3.

Row 2 and all even rows: Purl.

Row 3: K7, YO, sl 1, K1, psso, K2.

Row 5: K3, K2tog, YO, K3, YO, sl 1, K1, psso, K1.

Row 7: K2, K2tog, YO, K5, YO, sl 1, K1, psso.

Row 9: K1, K2tog, YO, K8.

Row 11: K2tog, YO, K9.

Row 12: Purl.

Rep rows 1–12 for patt.

Fish-Scale Lace Panel

Worked over 17 sts on a background of St st

Row 1 (RS): K1, YO, K3, sl 1, K1, psso, P5, K2tog, K3, YO, K1.

Row 2: P6, K5, P6.

Row 3: K2, YO, K3, sl 1, K1, psso, P3, K2tog, K3, YO, K2.

Row 4: P7, K3, P7.

Row 5: K3, YO, K3, sl 1, K1, psso, P1, K2tog, K3, YO, K3.

Row 6: P8, K1, P8.

Row 7: K4, YO, K3, sl 1, K2tog, psso, K3, YO, K4.

Row 8: Purl.

Rep rows 1–8 for patt.

Single-Eyelet Rib

Multiple of 5 + 2

Row 1 (RS): P2, *K3, P2; rep from * to end.

Row 2: K2, *P3, K2; rep from * to end.

Row 3: P2, *K2tog, YO, K1, P2; rep from * to end.

Row 4: Rep row 2.

Rows 5 and 6: Rep rows 1 and 2.

Row 7: P2, *K1, YO, sl 1, K1, psso, P2; rep from * to end.

Row 8: Rep row 2.

Rep rows 1–8 for patt.

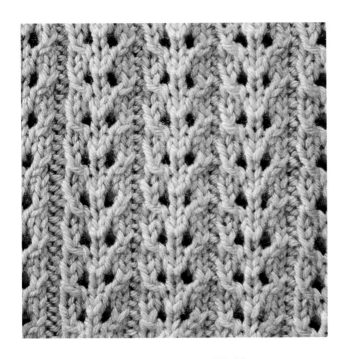

Double-Eyelet Rib

Multiple of 7 + 2

Row 1 (RS): P2, *K5, P2; rep from * to end.

Row 2: K2, *P5, K2; rep from * to end.

Row 3: P2, *K2tog, YO, K1, YO, sl 1, K1, psso, P2; rep from * to end.

Row 4: Rep row 2.

Rep rows 1–4 for patt.

Open Chain Rib

Multiple of 6 + 2

Row 1: K2, *P4, K2; rep from * to end.

Row 2 (RS): P2, *K2tog, YO twice, sl 1, K1, psso, P2; rep from * to end.

Row 3: K2, *P1, purl into front of first YO, purl into back of second YO, P1, K2; rep from * to end.

Row 4: P2, *YO, sl 1, K1, psso, K2tog, YO, P2; rep from * to end.

Rep rows 1–4 for patt.

Single Lace Rib

Multiple of 4 + 1

Row 1 (RS): K1, *YO, K2tog, P1, K1; rep from * to end.

Row 2: P1, *YO, P2tog, K1, P1; rep from * to end.

Rep rows 1 and 2 for patt.

Garter-Stitch Eyelet Chevron

Multiple of 9 + 1

Row 1 (RS): K1, *YO, sl 1, K1, psso, K4, K2tog, YO, K1; rep from * to end.

Row 2: P2, *K6, P3; rep from * to last 8 sts, K6, P2.

Row 3: K2, *YO, sl 1, K1, psso, K2, K2tog, YO, K3; rep from * to last 8 sts, YO, sl 1, K1, psso, K2, K2tog, YO, K2.

Row 4: P3, *K4, P5; rep from * to last 7 sts, K4, P3.

Row 5: K3, *YO, sl 1, K1, psso, K2tog, YO, K5; rep from * to last 7 sts, YO, sl 1, K1, psso, K2tog, YO, K3.

Row 6: P4, *K2, P7; rep from * to last 6 sts, K2, P4.

Rep rows 1–6 for patt.

Fern Lace

Multiple of 9 + 4

Row 1: Purl.

Row 2 (RS): K3, *YO, K2, sl 1, K1, psso, K2tog, K2, YO, K1; rep from * to last st, K1.

Row 3: Purl.

Row 4: K2, *YO, K2, sl 1, K1, psso, K2tog, K2, YO, K1; rep from * to last 2 sts, K2.

Rep rows 1–4 for patt.

Lacy Diamonds

Multiple of 6 + 1

Row 1 (RS): *K1, K2tog, YO, K1, YO, K2tog through back loop; rep from * to last st, K1.

Row 2 and all even rows: Purl.

Row 3: K2tog, *YO, K3, YO, sl 1 twice, K1, p2sso; rep from * to last 5 sts, YO, K3, YO, K2tog through back loop.

Row 5: *K1, YO, K2tog through back loop, K1, K2tog, YO; rep from * to last st, K1.

Row 7: K2, *YO, sl 1 twice, K1, p2sso, YO, K3; rep from * to last 5 sts, YO, sl 1 twice, K1, p2sso, YO, K2.

Row 8: Purl.

Rep rows 1–8 for patt.

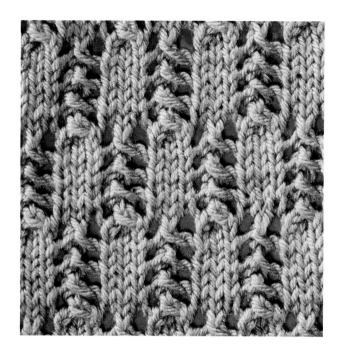 

Alternating Lace

Multiple of 6 + 5

Row 1 (RS): K1, *YO, sl 1, K2tog, psso, YO, K3; rep from * to last 4 sts, YO, sl 1, K2tog, psso, YO, K1.

Row 2: Purl.

Rows 3–8: Rep rows 1 and 2 three more times.

Row 9: K4, *YO, sl 1, K2tog, psso, YO, K3; rep from * to last st, K1.

Row 10: Purl.

Rows 11–16: Rep rows 9 and 10 three more times.

Rep rows 1–16 for patt.

Lace Check

Multiple of 18 + 9

Row 1: Purl.

Row 2 (RS): K1, *(YO, K2tog) 4 times, K10; rep from * to last 8 sts, (YO, K2tog) 4 times.

Row 3: Purl.

Row 4: *(Sl 1, K1, psso, YO) 4 times, K10; rep from * to last 9 sts, (sl 1, K1, psso, YO) 4 times, K1.

Rows 5–12: Rep rows 1–4 twice.

Row 13: Purl.

Row 14: *K10, (YO, K2tog) 4 times; rep from * to last 9 sts, K9.

Row 15: Purl.

Row 16: K9, *(sl 1, K1, psso, YO) 4 times, K10; rep from * to end.

Rows 17–24: Rep rows 13–16 twice.

Rep rows 1–24 for patt.

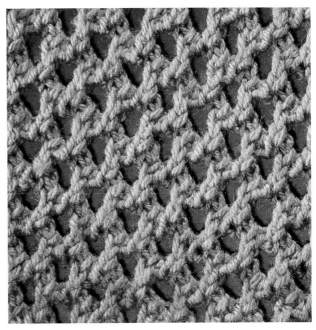

Faggoting

Multiple of 3

Row 1 (RS): *K1, YO twice, K2tog; rep from * to end.

Row 2: P1, *purl into first YO of previous row, drop 2nd YO off needle, P2; rep from * to last 3 sts, purl into first YO, drop 2nd YO off needle, P1.

Row 3: *K2tog, YO twice, K1; rep from * to end.

Row 4: Rep row 2.

Rep rows 1–4 for patt.

Fancy Openwork

Multiple of 4

Row 1 (RS): K2, *YO, K4; rep from * to last 2 sts, YO, K2.

Row 2: P2tog, *(K1, P1) into YO from previous row, P2tog twice; rep from * to last 3 sts, (K1, P1) into YO from previous row, P2tog.

Row 3: K4, *YO, K4; rep from * to end.

Row 4: P2, P2tog, *(K1, P1) into YO from previous row, P2tog twice; rep from * to last 5 sts, (K1, P1) into YO from previous row, P2tog, P2.

Rep rows 1–4 for patt.

Bell Lace

Multiple of 8 + 3

Row 1 (RS): K1, P1, K1, *P1, YO, sl 1, K2tog, psso, YO, (P1, K1) twice; rep from * to end.

Row 2: P1, K1, P1, *K1, P3, (K1, P1) twice; rep from * to end.

Rows 3–6: Rep rows 1 and 2 twice.

Row 7: K1, K2tog, *YO, (P1, K1) twice, P1, YO, sl 1, K2tog, psso; rep from * to last 8 sts, YO, (P1, K1) twice, P1, YO, sl 1, K1, psso, K1.

Row 8: P3, *(K1, P1) twice, K1, P3; rep from * to end.

Rows 9–12: Rep rows 7 and 8 twice.

Rep rows 1–12 for patt.

Diamond Rib

Multiple of 9 + 2

Row 1 (RS): P2, *K2tog, (K1, YO) twice, K1, sl 1, K1, psso, P2; rep from * to end.

Row 2 and all even rows: K2, *P7, K2; rep from * to end.

Row 3: P2, *K2tog, YO, K3, YO, sl 1, K1, psso, P2; rep from * to end.

Row 5: P2, *K1, YO, sl 1, K1, psso, K1, K2tog, YO, K1, P2; rep from * to end.

Row 7: P2, *K2, YO, sl 1, K2tog, psso, YO, K2, P2; rep from * to end.

Row 8: Rep row 2.

Rep rows 1–8 for patt.

Gate and Ladder Pattern

Multiple of 9 + 3

Row 1: Purl.

Row 2 (RS): K1, K2tog, K3, YO twice, K3, *K3tog, K3, YO twice, K3; rep from * to last 3 sts, K2tog, K1.

Row 3: P6, K1, *P8, K1; rep from * to last 5 sts, P5.

Rep rows 2 and 3 for patt.

Little Shell Insertion

Worked over 7 sts on a background of St st

Row 1 (RS): Knit.

Row 2: Purl.

Row 3: K1, YO, P1, P3tog, P1, YO, K1.

Row 4: Purl.

Rep rows 1–4 for patt.

Eyelet Lattice Insertion

Worked over 8 sts on a background of St st

Row 1 (RS): K1, (K2tog, YO) 3 times, K1.

Row 2: Purl.

Row 3: K2, (K2tog, YO) twice, K2.

Row 4: Purl.

Rep rows 1–4 for patt.

Allover Eyelets

Multiple of 10 + 1

Row 1 (RS): Knit.

Row 2 and all even rows: Purl.

Row 3: K3, * K2tog, YO, K1, YO, sl 1, K1, psso, K5; rep from * to last 8 sts, K2tog, YO, K1, YO, sl 1, K1, psso, K3.

Row 5: Knit.

Row 7: K1, *YO, sl 1, K1, psso, K5, K2tog, YO, K1; rep from * to end.

Row 8: Purl.

Rep rows 1–8 for patt.

Eyelet Lace

Multiple of 6 + 2

Row 1 (RS): K1, YO, *K2tog through back loop, K2, K2tog, YO; rep from * to last st, K1.

Row 2: K1, P5, * purl into front and back of next st, P4; rep from * to last 2 sts, P1, K1.

Row 3: K2, *K2tog, YO, K2tog through back loop, K2; rep from * to end.

Row 4: K1, P2, *purl into front and back of next st, P4; rep from * to last 4 sts, purl into front and back of next st, P2, K1.

Rep rows 1–4 for patt.

Eyelet Twigs

Worked over 14 sts on a background of St st

Row 1 (RS): K1, YO, K3tog, YO, K3, YO, sl 1, K2tog, psso, YO, K4.

Row 2 and all even rows: Purl.

Row 3: YO, K3tog, YO, K5, YO, sl 1, K2tog, psso, YO, K3.

Row 5: K5, YO, K3tog, YO, K1, YO, sl 1, K2tog, psso, YO, K2.

Row 7: K4, YO, K3tog, YO, K3, YO, sl 1, K2tog, psso, YO, K1.

Row 9: K3, YO, K3tog, YO, K5, YO, sl 1, K2tog, psso, YO.

Row 11: K2, YO, K3tog, YO, K1, YO, sl 1, K2tog, psso, YO, K5.

Row 12: Purl.

Rep rows 1–12 for patt.

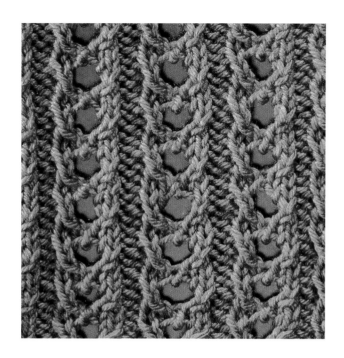 

Large Eyelet Rib

Multiple of 6 + 2

Row 1 (RS): *P2, K2tog, YO twice, sl 1, K1, psso; rep from * to last 2 sts, P2.

Row 2: K2, *P1, K1, P2, K2; rep from * to end.

Row 3: *P2, K4; rep from * to last 2 sts, P2.

Row 4: K2, *P4, K2; rep from * to end.

Rep rows 1–4 for patt.

Eyelet Rib

Multiple of 11 + 4

Row 1 (RS): K1, YO, P2tog, K1, *P1, K2, YO, sl 1, K1, psso, K1, P1, K1, YO, P2tog, K1; rep from * to end.

Row 2 and all even rows: K1, YO, P2tog, *K2, P5, K2, YO, P2tog; rep from * to last st, K1.

Row 3: K1, YO, P2tog, K1, *P1, K1, YO, sl 1, K2tog, psso, YO, K1, P1, K1, YO, P2tog, K1; rep from * to end.

Row 5: Rep row 1.

Row 7: K1, YO, P2tog, K1, *P1, K5, P1, K1, YO, P2tog, K1; rep from * to end.

Row 8: Rep row 2.

Rep rows 1–8 for patt.

Chevron Rib 2

Multiple of 7 + 2

Row 1 (RS): K2, *K2tog, YO, K1, YO, sl 1, K1, psso, K2; rep from * to end.

Row 2: Purl.

Row 3: K1, * K2tog, YO, K3, YO, sl 1, K1, psso; rep from * to last st, K1.

Row 4: Purl.

Rep rows 1–4 for patt.

Scallop Pattern

Multiple of 13 + 2

Row 1 (RS): K1, *sl 1, K1, psso, K9, K2tog; rep from * to last st, K1.

Row 2: Purl.

Row 3: K1, *sl 1, K1, psso, K7, K2tog; rep from * to last st, K1.

Row 4: Purl.

Row 5: K1, *sl 1, K1, psso, YO, (K1, YO) 5 times, K2tog; rep from * to last st, K1.

Row 6: Knit.

Rep rows 1–6 for patt.

Ridged Lace 2

Multiple of 2

Row 1 (RS): K1, *YO, K2tog through back
loop; rep from * to last st, K1.

Row 2: P1, *YO, P2tog; rep from * to last st, P1.

Rep rows 1 and 2 for patt.

Foaming Waves

Multiple of 12 + 1

Rows 1–4: Knit.

Row 5 (RS): K1, *K2tog twice, (YO, K1) 3 times,
YO, (sl 1, K1, psso) twice, K1; rep from * to
end.

Row 6: Purl.

Rows 7–12: Rep rows 5 and 6 three more times.

Rep rows 1–12 for patt.

Arch Lace Panel

Worked over 11 sts on a background of St st

Row 1 (RS): K1, YO, K2tog, K5, sl 1, K1, psso, YO, K1.

Row 2 and all even rows: Purl.

Row 3: Rep row 1.

Row 5: Rep row 1.

Row 7: K1, YO, K3, sl 1, K2tog, psso, K3, YO, K1.

Row 9: K2, YO, K2, sl 1, K2tog, psso, K2, YO, K2.

Row 11: K3, YO, K1, sl 1, K2tog, psso, K1, YO, K3.

Row 13: K4, YO, sl 1, K2tog, psso, YO, K4.

Row 14: Purl.

Rep rows 1–14 for patt.

Lace Rib Panel

Worked over 7 sts on a background of reverse St st

Row 1 (RS): P1, YO, sl 1, K1, psso, K1, K2tog, YO, P1.

Row 2: K1, P5, K1.

Row 3: P1, K1, YO, sl 1, K2tog, psso, YO, K1, P1.

Row 4: K1, P5, K1.

Rep rows 1–4 for patt.

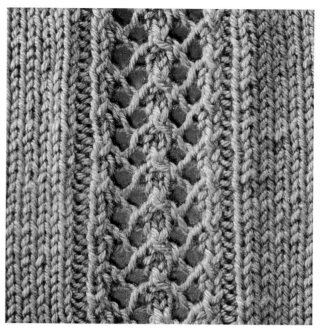

Fan Lace Panel

Worked over 11 sts on a background of St st

Row 1 (RS): Sl 1, K1, psso, K next 3 sts through back loop, YO, K1, YO, K next 3 sts through back loop, K2tog.

Row 2 and all even rows: Purl.

Row 3: Sl 1, K1, psso, K next 2 sts through back loop, YO, K1, YO, sl 1, K1, psso, YO, K next 2 sts through back loop, K2tog.

Row 5: Sl 1, K1, psso, K1 through back loop, YO, K1, (YO, sl 1, K1, psso) twice, YO, K1 through back loop, K2tog.

Row 7: Sl 1, K1, psso, YO, K1, (YO, sl 1, K1, psso) 3 times, YO, K2tog.

Row 8: Purl.

Rep rows 1–8 for patt.

Open-Weave Panel

Worked over 11 sts on a background of St st

Row 1 (RS): P2, sl 1 wyib, K1, psso, YO, K3, YO, K2tog, P2.

Row 2: K2, P7, K2.

Row 3: P2, K2, YO, sl 1, K2tog, psso, YO, K2, P2.

Row 4: K2, P7, K2.

Rep rows 1–4 for patt.

Lacy Zigzag

Multiple of 6 + 1

Row 1 (RS): *Sl 1, K1, psso, K2, YO, K2; rep from * to last st, K1.

Row 2: Purl.

Rows 3–6: Rep rows 1 and 2 twice.

Row 7: K3, *YO, K2, K2tog, K2; rep from * to last 4 sts, YO, K2, K2tog.

Row 8: Purl.

Rows 9–12: Rep rows 7 and 8 twice.

Rep rows 1–12 for patt.

Climbing Leaf Pattern

Multiple of 16 + 1

Row 1 (RS): K1, *YO, K5, K2tog, K1, K2tog through back loop, K5, YO, K1; rep from * to end.

Row 2 and all even rows: Purl.

Row 3: Rep row 1.

Row 5: K1, *K2tog through back loop, K5, YO, K1, YO, K5, K2tog, K1; rep from * to end.

Row 7: Rep row 5.

Row 8: Purl.

Rep rows 1–8 for patt.

Arrowhead Lace

Multiple of 10 + 1

Row 1 (RS): K1, *(YO, sl 1, K1, psso) twice, K1, (K2tog, YO) twice, K1; rep from * to end.

Row 2: Purl.

Row 3: K2, *YO, sl 1, K1, psso, YO, sl 1, K2tog, psso, YO, K2tog, YO, K3; rep from * to last 9 sts, YO, sl 1, K1, psso, YO, sl 1, K2tog, psso, YO, K2tog, YO, K2.

Row 4: Purl.

Rep rows 1–4 for patt.

Purse Stitch

Multiple of 2

All rows: P1, *YO, P2tog; rep from * to last st, P1.

Rep row for patt.

Simple Garter-Stitch Lace

Multiple of 4 + 2

All rows: K2, *YO, P2tog, K2; rep from * to end.

Rep row for patt.

Lacy Openwork

Multiple of 4 + 1

Row 1 (RS): K1, *YO, P3tog, YO, K1; rep from * to end.

Row 2: P2tog, YO, K1, YO, *P3tog, YO, K1, YO; rep from * to last 2 sts, P2tog.

Rep rows 1 and 2 for patt.

Open-Check Stitch

Multiple of 2

Row 1 (RS): Purl.

Row 2: Knit.

Row 3: K2, *sl 1, K1; rep from * to end.

Row 4: *K1, sl 1 wyif; rep from * to last 2 sts, K2.

Row 5: K1, *YO, K2tog; rep from * to last st, K1.

Row 6: Purl.

Rep rows 1–6 for patt.

Feather Rib

Multiple of 5 + 2

Row 1 (RS): P2, *YO, K2tog through back loop, K1, P2; rep from * to end.

Row 2: K2, *YO, K2tog through back loop, P1, K2; rep from * to end.

Rep rows 1 and 2 for patt.

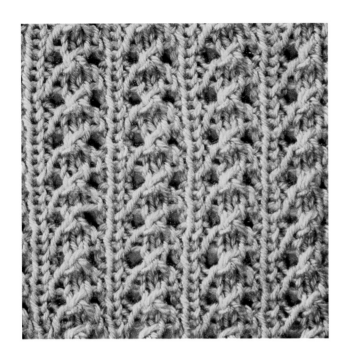

Perforated Ribbing

Multiple of 6 + 3

Row 1 (RS): P1, K1, P1, *YO, P3tog, YO, P1, K1, P1; rep from * to end.

Row 2: K1, P1, K1, *P3, K1, P1, K1; rep from * to end.

Row 3: P1, K1, P1, *K3, P1, K1, P1; rep from * to end.

Row 4: Rep row 2.

Rep rows 1–4 for patt.

Staggered Fern Lace Panel

Worked over 20 sts on a background of St st

Row 1 (RS): P2, K9, YO, K1, YO, K3, sl 1, K2tog, psso, P2.

Row 2 and all even rows: Purl.

Row 3: P2, K10, YO, K1, YO, K2, sl 1, K2tog, psso, P2.

Row 5: P2, K3tog, K4, YO, K1, YO, K3, (YO, K1) twice, sl 1, K2tog, psso, P2.

Row 7: P2, K3tog, K3, YO, K1, YO, K9, P2.

Row 9: P2, K3tog, K2, YO, K1, YO, K10, P2.

Row 11: P2, K3tog, (K1, YO) twice, K3, YO, K1, YO, K4, sl 1, K2tog, psso, P2.

Row 12: Purl.

Rep rows 1–12 for patt.

Shetland Eyelet Panel

Worked over 9 sts on a background of St st

Row 1 (RS): K2, K2tog, YO, K1, YO, sl 1, K1, psso, K2.

Row 2 and all even rows: Purl.

Row 3: K1, K2tog, YO, K3, YO, sl 1, K1, psso, K1.

Row 5: K1, YO, sl 1, K1, psso, YO, sl 2 knitwise, K1, p2sso, YO, K2tog, YO, K1.

Row 7: K3, YO, sl 2 knitwise, K1, p2sso, YO, K3.

Row 8: Purl.

Rep rows 1–8 for patt.

Traveling Ribbed Eyelet Panel

Worked over 13 sts on a background of St st

Row 1 (RS): K2, P2, YO, sl 1, K1, psso, K1, K2tog, YO, P2, K2.

Row 2: K4, P5, K4.

Rows 3–6: Rep rows 1 and 2 twice.

Row 7: K2, P2, K5, P2, K2.

Row 8: Rep row 2.

Row 9: K2, P2, K2tog, YO, K1, YO, sl 1, K1, psso, P2, K2.

Row 10: Rep row 2.

Rows 11–14: Rep rows 9 and 10 twice.

Row 15: Rep row 7.

Row 16: Rep row 2.

Rep rows 1–16 for patt.

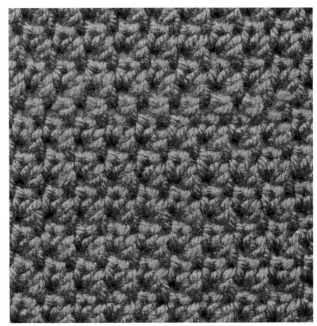

Little Shell Pattern

Multiple of 7 + 2

Row 1 (RS): Knit.

Row 2: Purl.

Row 3: K2, *YO, P1, P3tog, P1, YO, K2; rep from * to end.

Row 4: Purl.

Rep rows 1–4 for patt.

Zigzag Openwork

Multiple of 2 + 1

Row 1 (RS): K1, *K2tog; rep from * to end.

Row 2: K1, *YO, K1; rep from * to end.

Row 3: *K2tog; rep from * to last st, K1.

Row 4: Rep row 2.

Rep rows 1–4 for patt.

Whelk Pattern

Multiple of 4 + 3

Row 1 (RS): K3, *sl 1 wyib, K3; rep from * to end.

Row 2: K3, *sl 1 wyif, K3; rep from * to end.

Row 3: K1, *sl 1 wyib, K3; rep from * to last 2 sts, sl 1 wyib, K1.

Row 4: P1, sl 1 wyif, *P3, sl 1 wyif; rep from * to last st, P1.

Rep rows 1–4 for patt.

Eyelet Knot Stitch

Multiple of 2

Row 1 (RS): K1, *K2tog; rep from * to last st, K1.

Row 2: K2, *M1, K1; rep from * to end.

Row 3: Knit.

Row 4: Purl.

Rep rows 1–4 for patt.

Rose-Hip Stitch

Multiple of 4 + 3

Row 1 (RS): K3, *sl 1 wyib, K3; rep from * to end.

Row 2: K3, *sl 1 wyif, K3; rep from * to end.

Row 3: K1, *sl 1 wyib, K3; rep from * to last 2 sts, sl 1 wyib, K1.

Row 4: K1, *sl 1 wyif, K3; rep from * to last 2 sts, sl 1 wyif, K1.

Rep rows 1–4 for patt.

Chevron

Multiple of 8 + 1

Row 1 (RS): K1, *P7, K1; rep from * to end.

Row 2: P1, *K7, P1; rep from * to end.

Row 3: K2, *P5, K3; rep from * to last 7 sts, P5, K2.

Row 4: P2, *K5, P3; rep from * to last 7 sts, K5, P2.

Row 5: K3, *P3, K5; rep from * to last 6 sts, P3, K3.

Row 6: P3, *K3, P5; rep from * to last 6 sts, K3, P3.

Row 7: K4, *P1, K7; rep from * to last 5 sts, P1, K4.

Row 8: P4, *K1, P7; rep from * to last 5 sts, K1, P4.

Row 9: Rep row 2.

Row 10: Rep row 1.

Row 11: Rep row 4.

Row 12: Rep row 3.

Row 13: Rep row 6.

Row 14: Rep row 5.

Row 15: Rep row 8.

Row 16: Rep row 7.

Rep rows 1–16 for patt.

Knotted Cords

Multiple of 6 + 5

Row 1 (RS): P5, *K1, P5; rep from * to end.

Row 2: K5, *P1, K5; rep from * to end.

Row 3: P5, *knit into front, back, and front of next st, P5; rep from * to end.

Row 4: K5, *P3tog, K5; rep from * to end.

Rep rows 1–4 for patt.

Organ Pipes

Multiple of 6 + 4

Row 1 (RS): K4, *P2, K4; rep from * to end.

Row 2: P4, *K2, P4; rep from * to end.

Row 3: Rep row 1.

Row 4: Rep row 2.

Row 5: P1, K2, *P4, K2; rep from * to last st, P1.

Row 6: K1, P2, *K4, P2; rep from * to last st, K1.

Row 7: Rep row 5.

Row 8: Rep row 6.

Row 9: Purl.

Row 10: Knit.

Rep rows 1–10 for patt.

Diagonal Crossed Stitch

Multiple of 2

Row 1: K1, *sl 1, K1, YO, psso the K1 and YO; rep from * to last st, K1.

Row 2: Purl.

Row 3: K2, *sl 1, K1, YO, psso the K1 and YO; rep from * to end.

Row 4: Purl.

Rep rows 1–4 for patt.

Horizontal Two-One Ribs

Multiple of 3 + 1

Rows 1–4: Work 4 rows of St st, beginning with a knit row.

Row 5: K1, *P2, K1; rep from * to end.

Row 6: *K1, P2; rep from * to last st, K1.

Row 7: P1, *K2, P1; rep from * to end.

Rows 8–12: Work 5 rows of St st, beginning with a purl row.

Rep rows 1–12 for patt.

Garter-Stitch Chevron

Multiple of 11

Rows 1–5: Using color A, knit.

Row 6 (RS): Using color B, *K2tog, K2, knit into front and back of next 2 sts, K3, sl 1, K1, psso; rep from * to end.

Row 7: Using color B, purl.

Rows 8–11: Rep rows 6 and 7 twice.

Row 12: Work row 6, using color A instead of color B.

Rep rows 1–12 for patt.

Piqué Check Stitch

Multiple of 6

Rows 1–6: Work 6 rows of St st, beginning with a knit row.

Row 7: *K3, P3; rep from * to end.

Row 8: Purl.

Row 9: Rep row 7.

Row 10: Purl.

Row 11: Rep row 7.

Rows 12–18: Work 7 rows of St st, beginning with a purl row.

Row 19: *P3, K3; rep from * to end.

Row 20: Purl.

Row 21: Rep row 19.

Row 22: Purl.

Row 23: Rep row 19.

Row 24: Purl.

Rep rows 1–24 for patt.

Rectangular Checks

Multiple of 6

Row 1 and all odd rows (RS): Knit.

Rows 2, 4, 6, 8, 10, and 12: *K3, P3; rep from
* to end.

Rows 14, 16, 18, 20, 22, and 24: *P3, K3; rep
from * to end.

Rep rows 1–24 for patt.

Garter Stitch

Knit all rows.

Stockinette Stitch

Row 1 (RS): Knit.

Row 2: Purl.

Rep rows 1 and 2 for patt.

Reverse Stockinette Stitch

Row 1 (RS): Purl.

Row 2: Knit.

Rep rows 1 and 2 for patt.

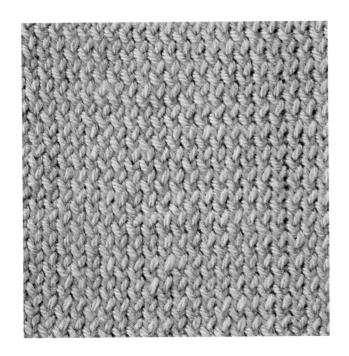

Crossed Stockinette Stitch

Row 1 (RS): Knit, working into the back of each st.

Row 2: Purl.

Rep rows 1 and 2 for patt.

Seed Stitch 1

Odd number of stitches: Multiple of 2 + 1

Row 1: K1, *P1, K1; rep from * to end.

Rep row 1 for patt.

Even number of stitches: Multiple of 2

Row 1: *K1, P1; rep from * to end.

Row 2: *P1, K1; rep from * to end.

Rep rows 1 and 2 for patt.

Moss Stitch

Even number of stitches

Rows 1 and 2: *K1, P1; rep from * to end.

Rows 3 and 4: *P1, K1; rep from * to end.

Rep rows 1–4 for patt.

Box Stitch

Multiple of 4 + 2

Row 1: K2, *P2, K2; rep from * to end.

Row 2: P2, *K2, P2; rep from * to end.

Row 3: Rep row 2.

Row 4: Rep row 1.

Rep rows 1–4 for patt.

Fleck Stitch

Multiple of 2 + 1

Row 1 (RS): Knit.

Row 2: Purl.

Row 3: K1, *P1, K1; rep from * to end.

Row 4: Purl.

Rep rows 1–4 for patt.

Double Fleck Stitch

Multiple of 6 + 4

Row 1 (RS): Knit.

Row 2: P4, *K2, P4; rep from * to end.

Row 3: Knit.

Row 4: P1, *K2, P4; rep from * to last 3 sts, K2, P1.

Rep rows 1–4 for patt.

Broken-Rib Diagonal

Multiple of 6

Row 1 (RS): *K4, P2; rep from * to end.

Row 2: *K2, P4; rep from * to end.

Row 3: Rep row 1.

Row 4: Rep row 2.

Row 5: K2, *P2, K4; rep from * to last 4 sts, P2, K2.

Row 6: P2, *K2, P4; rep from * to last 4 sts, K2, P2.

Rows 7 and 8: Rep rows 5 and 6.

Row 9: *P2, K4; rep from * to end.

Row 10: *P4, K2; rep from * to end.

Rows 11 and 12: Rep rows 9 and 10.

Rep rows 1–12 for patt.

Lattice Stitch

Multiple of 6 + 1

Row 1 (RS): K3, *P1, K5; rep from * to last 4 sts, P1, K3.

Row 2: P2, *K1, P1, K1, P3; rep from * to last 5 sts, K1, P1, K1, P2.

Row 3: K1, *P1, K3, P1, K1; rep from * to end.

Row 4: K1, *P5, K1; rep from * to end.

Row 5: Rep row 3.

Row 6: Rep row 2.

Rep rows 1–6 for patt.

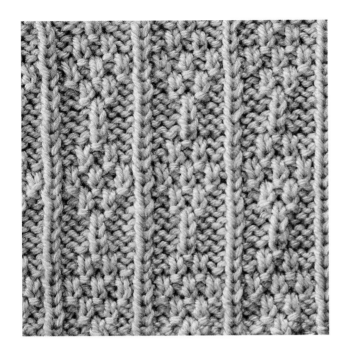

Moss Panels

Multiple of 8 + 7

Row 1: K3, *P1, K3; rep from * to end.

Row 2 (RS): P3, *K1, P3; rep from * to end.

Row 3: K2, P1, K1, *(P1, K2) twice, P1, K1; rep from * to last 3 sts, P1, K2.

Row 4: P2, K1, P1, *(K1, P2) twice, K1, P1; rep from * to last 3 sts, K1, P2.

Row 5: K1, *P1, K1; rep from * to end.

Row 6: P1, *K1, P1; rep from * to end.

Row 7: Rep row 3.

Row 8: Rep row 4.

Row 9: Rep row 1.

Row 10: Rep row 2.

Rep rows 1–10 for patt.

Dot Stitch

Multiple of 4 + 3

Row 1 (RS): K1, *P1, K3; rep from * to last 2 sts, P1, K1.

Row 2: Purl.

Row 3: *K3, P1; rep from * to last 3 sts, K3.

Row 4: Purl.

Rep rows 1–4 for patt.

Purled Ladder Stitch

Multiple of 4 + 2

Rows 1 and 2: Knit.

Row 3 (RS): P2, *K2, P2; rep from * to end.

Row 4: K2, *P2, K2; rep from * to end.

Rows 5 and 6: Knit.

Row 7: Rep row 4.

Row 8: P2, *K2, P2; rep from * to end.

Rep rows 1–8 for patt.

Diamond Panels

Multiple of 8 + 1

Row 1 (RS): Knit.

Row 2: K1, *P7, K1; rep from * to end.

Row 3: K4, *P1, K7; rep from * to last 5 sts, P1, K4.

Row 4: K1, *P2, K1, P1, K1, P2, K1; rep from * to end.

Row 5: K2, *(P1, K1) twice, P1, K3; rep from * to last 7 sts, (P1, K1) twice, P1, K2.

Row 6: Rep row 4.

Row 7: Rep row 3.

Row 8: Rep row 2.

Rep rows 1–8 for patt.

Tile Stitch

Multiple of 6 + 4

Row 1 (RS): K4, *P2, K4; rep from * to end.

Row 2: P4, *K2, P4; rep from * to end.

Rows 3–6: Rep rows 1 and 2 twice more.

Row 7: Rep row 2.

Row 8: K4, *P2, K4; rep from * to end.

Rep rows 1–8 for patt.

Steps

Multiple of 8 + 2

Row 1 (RS): *K4, P4; rep from * to last 2 sts, K2.

Row 2: P2, *K4, P4; rep from * to end.

Rows 3 and 4: Rep rows 1 and 2.

Row 5: K2, *P4, K4; rep from * to end.

Row 6: *P4, K4; rep from * to last 2 sts, P2.

Rows 7 and 8: Rep rows 5 and 6.

Row 9: Rep row 6.

Rows 10 and 11: Rep rows 5 and 6.

Row 12: Rep row 5.

Row 13: Rep row 2

Rows 14 and 15: Rep rows 1 and 2.

Row 16: Rep row 1.

Rep rows 1–16 for patt.

Garter-Stitch Steps

Multiple of 8

Row 1 and all odd rows (RS): Knit.

Row 2: *K4, P4; rep from * to end.

Row 4: Rep row 2.

Row 6: K2, *P4, K4; rep from * to last 6 sts, P4, K2.

Row 8: Rep row 6.

Row 10: *P4, K4; rep from * to end.

Row 12: Rep row 10.

Row 14: P2, *K4, P4; rep from * to last 6 sts, K4, P2.

Row 16: Rep row 14.

Rep rows 1–16 for patt.

Diagonal Checks

Multiple of 5

Row 1 (RS): *P1, K4; rep from * to end.

Row 2: *P3, K2; rep from * to end.

Row 3: Rep row 2.

Row 4: Rep row 1.

Row 5: *K1, P4; rep from * to end.

Row 6: *K3, P2; rep from * to end.

Row 7: Rep row 6.

Row 8: Rep row 5.

Rep rows 1–8 for patt.

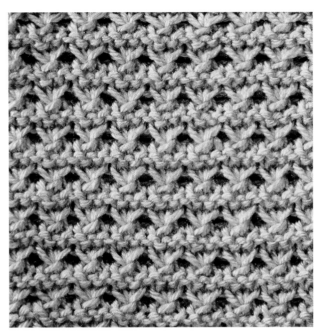

Stockinette Ridge

Multiple of 2

Row 1 (RS): Knit.

Row 2: P1, *K2tog; rep from * to last st, P1.

Row 3: K1, *knit into front and back of next st; rep from * to last st, K1.

Row 4: Purl.

Rep rows 1–4 for patt.

Ridged Knot Stitch

Multiple of 3 + 2

Row 1 (RS): Knit.

Row 2: K1, *MK; rep from * to last st, K1.

Rows 3 and 4: Knit.

Rep rows 1–4 for patt.

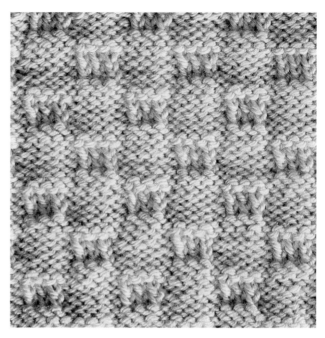

Alternating Triangles

Multiple of 5

Row 1 (RS): *P1, K4; rep from * to end.

Rows 2 and 3: *P3, K2; rep from * to end.

Row 4: Rep row 1.

Row 5: *K4, P1; rep from * to end.

Rows 6 and 7: *K2, P3; rep from * to end.

Row 8: Rep row 5.

Rep rows 1–8 for patt.

Twisted Check Pattern

Multiple of 8 + 5

Row 1 (RS): Purl.

Row 2: K1, *P next 3 sts through back loop, K5; rep from * to last 4 sts, P next 3 sts through back loop, K1.

Row 3: P1, *K next 3 sts through back loop, P5; rep from * to last 4 sts, K next 3 sts through back loop, P1.

Row 4: Rep row 2.

Row 5: Purl.

Row 6: Knit.

Row 7: P5, *K next 3 sts through back loop, P5; rep from * to end.

Row 8: K5, *P next 3 sts through back loop, K5; rep from * to end.

Row 9: Rep row 7.

Row 10: Knit.

Rep rows 1–10 for patt.

Stockinette Triangles

Multiple of 5

Row 1 (RS): Knit.

Row 2: *K1, P4; rep from * to end.

Row 3: *K3, P2; rep from * to end.

Row 4: Rep row 3.

Row 5: Rep row 2.

Row 6: Knit.

Rep rows 1–6 for patt.

Pillar Stitch

Multiple of 2

Row 1: Purl.

Row 2 (RS): K1, *YO, K2, pass YO over K2; rep from * to last st, K1.

Rep rows 1 and 2 for patt.

Moss-Stitch Squares

Multiple of 12 + 3

Row 1 (RS): Knit.

Row 2: Purl.

Row 3: K4, *(P1, K1) 3 times, P1, K5; rep from * to last 11 sts, (P1, K1) 3 times, P1, K4.

Row 4: P3, *(K1, P1) 4 times, K1, P3; rep from * to end.

Row 5: K4, *P1, K5; rep from * to last 5 sts, P1, K4.

Row 6: P3, *K1, P7, K1, P3; rep from * to end.

Rows 7–11: Rep rows 5 and 6 twice more; then rep row 5 again.

Row 12: Rep row 4.

Row 13: Rep row 3.

Row 14: Purl.

Rep rows 1–14 for patt.

Textured Ribbing

Multiple of 6 + 3

Row 1: P3, *K3, P3; rep from * to end.

Row 2 (RS): K3, *P1, wyib, sl 1 knitwise, P1, K3; rep from * to end.

Rows 3–6: Rep rows 1 and 2 twice more.

Row 7: Knit.

Row 8: P4, *wyib, sl 1 knitwise, P5; rep from * to last 5 sts, wyib, sl 1 knitwise, P4.

Rep rows 1–8 for patt.

Raised Brick Stitch

Multiple of 4 + 3

Row 1 (RS): K3, *sl 1, K3; rep from * to end.

Row 2: K3, *sl 1 wyif, K3; rep from * to end.

Row 3: K1, sl 1, *K3, sl 1; rep from * to last st, K1.

Row 4: K1, sl 1 wyif, *K3, sl 1 wyif; rep from * to last st, K1.

Rep rows 1–4 for patt.

Diagonals

Multiple of 8 + 6

Row 1 (RS): P3, *K5, P3; rep from * to last 3 sts, K3.

Row 2: P4, *K3, P5, rep from * to last 2 sts, K2.

Row 3: P1, K5, *P3, K5; rep from * to end.

Row 4: K1, P5, *K3, P5; rep from * to end.

Row 5: K4, *P3, K5; rep from * to last 2 sts, P2.

Row 6: K3, *P5, K3; rep from * to last 3 sts, P3.

Row 7: K2, P3, *K5, P3; rep from * to last st, K1.

Row 8: P2, K3, *P5, K3; rep from * to last st, P1.

Rep rows 1–8 for patt.

Caterpillar Stitch

Multiple of 8 + 6

Row 1 (RS): K4, P2, *K6, P2; rep from * to end.

Row 2: P1, K2, *P6, K2; rep from * to last 3 sts, P3.

Row 3: K2, P2, *K6, P2; rep from * to last 2 sts, K2.

Row 4: P3, K2, *P6, K2; rep from * to last st, P1.

Row 5: P2, *K6, P2; rep from * to last 4 sts, K4.

Row 6: Purl.

Rep rows 1–6 for patt.

Diamond Pattern

Multiple of 8 + 1

Row 1 (RS): P1, *K7, P1; rep from * to end.

Row 2: K2, P5, *K3, P5; rep from * to last 2 sts, K2.

Row 3: K1, *P2, K3, P2, K1; rep from * to end.

Row 4: P2, K2, P1, K2, *P3, K2, P1, K2; rep from * to last 2 sts, P2.

Row 5: K3, P3, *K5, P3; rep from * to last 3 sts, K3.

Row 6: P4, K1, *P7, K1; rep from * to last 4 sts, P4.

Row 7: Rep row 5.

Row 8: Rep row 4.

Row 9: Rep row 3.

Row 10: Rep row 2.

Rep rows 1–10 for patt.

Little Arrows

Multiple of 8 + 1

Row 1 (RS): K2, P2, K1, P2, *K3, P2, K1, P2; rep from * to last 2 sts, K2.

Row 2: P3, K1, P1, K1, *P5, K1, P1, K1; rep from * to last 3 sts, P3.

Row 3: K1, *P1, K5, P1, K1; rep from * to end.

Row 4: P1, *K2, P3, K2, P1; rep from * to end.

Rep rows 1–4 for patt.

Banded Rib

Multiple of 2 + 1

Row 1 (RS): K1, *P1, K1; rep from * to end.

Row 2: P1, *K1, P1; rep from * to end.

Rows 3–6: Rep rows 1 and 2 twice more.

Row 7: P1, *K1, P1; rep from * to end.

Row 8: K1, *P1, K1; rep from * to end.

Rows 9–12: Rep rows 7 and 8 twice more.

Rep rows 1–12 for patt.

Double Basket Weave

Multiple of 4 + 3

Row 1 and all odd rows (RS): Knit.

Row 2: *K3, P1; rep from * to last 3 sts, K3.

Row 4: Rep row 2.

Row 6: K1, *P1, K3; rep from * to last 2 sts, P1, K1.

Row 8: Rep row 6.

Rep rows 1–8 for patt.

Woven Stitch 1

Multiple of 4 + 2

Row 1 (RS): Knit.

Row 2: Purl.

Row 3: K2, *P2, K2; rep from * to end.

Row 4: P2, *K2, P2; rep from * to end.

Row 5: Knit.

Row 6: Purl.

Row 7: Rep row 4.

Row 8: Rep row 3.

Rep rows 1–8 for patt.

Check Stitch

Multiple of 4 + 2

Row 1 (RS): K2, *P2, K2; rep from * to end.

Row 2: P2, *K2, P2; rep from * to end.

Rows 3 and 4: Rep rows 1 and 2.

Row 5: Rep row 2.

Rows 6 and 7: Rep rows 1 and 2.

Row 8: Rep row 1.

Rep rows 1–8 for patt.

Mosaic Stitch

Multiple of 10 + 7

Row 1 (RS): P3, *K1, P3, K1, P1, K1, P3; rep from * to last 4 sts, K1, P3.

Row 2: K3, *P1, K3, P1, K1, P1, K3; rep from * to last 4 sts, P1, K3.

Rows 3 and 4: Rep rows 1 and 2.

Row 5: P2, *K1, P1, K1, P3, K1, P3; rep from * to last 5 sts, K1, P1, K1, P2.

Row 6: K2, *P1, K1, P1, K3, P1, K3; rep from * to last 5 sts, P1, K1, P1, K2.

Rows 7 and 8: Rep rows 5 and 6.

Rep rows 1–8 for patt.

Ladder Stitch

Multiple of 8 + 5

Row 1 (RS): K5, *P3, K5; rep from * to end.

Row 2: P5, *K3, P5; rep from * to end.

Rows 3 and 4: Rep rows 1 and 2.

Row 5: K1, *P3, K5; rep from * to last 4 sts, P3, K1.

Row 6: P1, *K3, P5; rep from * to last 4 sts, K3, P1.

Rows 7 and 8: Rep rows 5 and 6.

Rep rows 1–8 for patt.

Pennant Stitch

Multiple of 5

Row 1 (RS): Knit.

Row 2: *K1, P4; rep from * to end.

Row 3: *K3, P2; rep from * to end.

Row 4: Rep row 3.

Row 5: Rep row 2.

Rows 6 and 7: Knit.

Row 8: *P4, K1; rep from * to end.

Row 9: *P2, K3; rep from * to end.

Row 10: Rep row 9.

Row 11: Rep row 8.

Row 12: Knit.

Rep rows 1–12 for patt.

Check Pattern

Multiple of 3 + 1

Row 1 (RS): Knit.

Row 2: Purl.

Row 3: K1, *P2, K1; rep from * to end.

Row 4: Purl.

Rep rows 1–4 for patt.

Close Checks

Multiple of 6 + 3

Row 1 (RS): K3, *P3, K3; rep from * to end.

Row 2: P3, *K3, P3; rep from * to end.

Rows 3 and 4: Rep rows 1 and 2.

Row 5: Rep row 2.

Rows 6 and 7: Rep rows 1 and 2.

Row 8: Rep row 1.

Rep rows 1–8 for patt.

Spaced Checks

Multiple of 10 + 1

Row 1: Purl.

Row 2 (RS): K4, *P3, K7; rep from * to last 7 sts, P3, K4.

Row 3: P4, *K3, P7; rep from * to last 7 sts, K3, P4.

Row 4: Rep row 2.

Row 5: Purl.

Row 6: Knit.

Row 7: K2, *P7, K3; rep from * to last 9 sts, P7, K2.

Row 8: P2, *K7, P3; rep from * to last 9 sts, K7, P2.

Row 9: Rep row 7.

Row 10: Knit.

Rep rows 1–10 for patt.

Rib Checks

Multiple of 10 + 5

Row 1 (RS): P5, *(K1 through back loop, P1) twice, K1 through back loop, P5; rep from * to end.

Row 2: K5, *(P1 through back loop, K1) twice, P1 through back loop, K5; rep from * to end.

Rows 3 and 4: Rep rows 1 and 2.

Row 5: Rep row 1.

Row 6: (P1 through back loop, K1) twice, P1 through back loop, *K5, (P1 through back loop, K1) twice, P1 through back loop; rep from * to end.

Row 7: (K1 through back loop, P1) twice, K1 through back loop, *P5, (K1 through back loop, P1) twice, K1 through back loop; rep from * to end.

Rows 8 and 9: Rep rows 6 and 7.

Row 10: Rep row 6.

Rep rows 1–10 for patt.

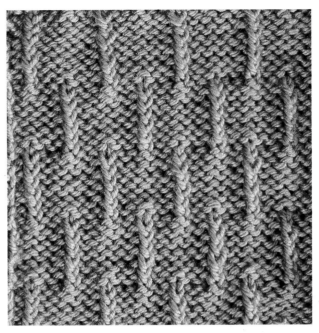

Piqué Triangles

Multiple of 5

Row 1 (RS): *P1, K4; rep from * to end.

Row 2: *P3, K2; rep from * to end.

Row 3: Rep row 2.

Row 4: Rep row 1.

Rep rows 1–4 for patt.

Dash Stitch

Multiple of 6 + 1

Row 1: K3, * P1 through back loop, K5; rep from * to last 4 sts, P1 through back loop, K3.

Row 2 (RS): P3, *K1 through back loop, P5; rep from * to last 4 sts, K1 through back loop, P3.

Rows 3–6: Rep rows 1 and 2 twice more.

Row 7: * P1 through back loop, K5; rep from * to last st, P1 through back loop.

Row 8: * K1 through back loop, P5; rep from * to last st, K1 through back loop.

Rows 9–12: Rep rows 7 and 8 twice more.

Rep rows 1–12 for patt.

Horizontal Dash Stitch

Multiple of 10 + 6

Row 1 (RS): P6, *K4, P6; rep from * to end.

Row 2 and all even rows: Purl.

Row 3: Knit.

Row 5: P1, *K4, P6; rep from * to last 5 sts, K4, P1.

Row 7: Knit.

Row 8: Purl.

Rep rows 1–8 for patt.

Squares

Multiple of 10 + 2

Row 1 (RS): Knit.

Row 2: Purl.

Row 3: K2, *P8, K2; rep from * to end.

Row 4: P2, *K8, P2; rep from * to end.

Row 5: K2, *P2, K4, P2, K2; rep from * to end.

Row 6: P2, *K2, P4, K2, P2; rep from * to end.

Rows 7–10: Rep rows 5 and 6 twice more.

Rows 11 and 12: Rep rows 3 and 4.

Rep rows 1–12 for patt.

Checkerboard

Multiple of 8 + 4

Row 1: K4, *P4, K4; rep from * to end.

Row 2: P4, *K4, P4; rep from * to end.

Rows 3 and 4: Rep rows 1 and 2.

Row 5: Rep row 2.

Rows 6 and 7: Rep rows 1 and 2.

Row 8: Rep row 1.

Rep rows 1–8 for patt.

Banded Basket Stitch

Multiple of 9 + 6

Row 1 (RS): P6, *K3, P6; rep from * to end.

Row 2: K6, *P3, K6; rep from * to end.

Rows 3–6: Rep rows 1 and 2 twice more.

Row 7: Rep row 2.

Rows 8 and 9: Rep rows 1 and 2.

Row 10: Rep row 1.

Rep rows 1–10 for patt.

Large Basket Weave

Multiple of 6 + 2

Row 1 (RS): Knit.

Row 2: Purl.

Row 3: K2, *P4, K2; rep from * to end.

Row 4: P2, *K4, P2; rep from * to end.

Rows 5 and 6: Rep rows 3 and 4.

Row 7: Knit.

Row 8: Purl.

Row 9: P3, *K2, P4; rep from * to last 5 sts, K2, P3.

Row 10: K3, *P2, K4; rep from * to last 5 sts, P2, K3.

Rows 11 and 12: Rep rows 9 and 10.

Rep rows 1–12 for patt.

Stockinette Checks

Multiple of 10 + 5

Row 1 (RS): K5, *P5, K5; rep from * to end.

Row 2: P5, *K5, P5; rep from * to end.

Rows 3 and 4: Rep rows 1 and 2.

Row 5: Rep row 1.

Rows 6–9: Rep rows 1 and 2 twice more.

Row 10: Rep row 1.

Rep rows 1–10 for patt.

Diagonal Seed Stitch

Multiple of 6

Row 1 (RS): *K5, P1; rep from * to end.

Row 2: P1,*K1, P5; rep from * to last 5 sts, K1, P4.

Row 3: K3, *P1, K5; rep from * to last 3 sts, P1, K2.

Row 4: P3, *K1, P5; rep from * to last 3 sts, K1, P2.

Row 5: K1, *P1, K5; rep from * to last 5 sts, P1, K4.

Row 6: *P5, K1; rep from * to end.

Rep rows 1–6 for patt.

Oblique Rib

Multiple of 4

Row 1 (RS): *K2, P2; rep from * to end.

Row 2: K1, *P2, K2; rep from * to last 3 sts, P2, K1.

Row 3: *P2, K2; rep from * to end.

Row 4: P1, *K2, P2; rep from * to last 3 sts, K2, P1.

Rep rows 1–4 for patt.

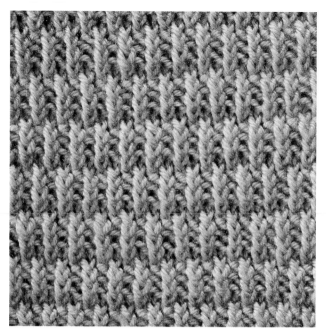

Tweed Pattern

Multiple of 6 + 3

Row 1 (RS): K3, *P3, K3; rep from * to end.

Rows 2 and 3: Rep row 1.

Row 4: Knit.

Row 5: Purl.

Row 6: Knit.

Rows 7–9: Rep row 1.

Row 10: Purl.

Row 11: Knit.

Row 12: Purl.

Rep rows 1–12 for patt.

Embossed Check Stitch

Multiple of 2 + 1

Row 1 (RS): K1 through back loop; rep from * to end.

Row 2: K1, *P1 through back loop, K1; rep from * to end.

Row 3: P1, *K1 through back loop, P1; rep from * to end.

Row 4: Rep row 2.

Row 5: Rep row 1.

Row 6: P1 through back loop, *K1, P1 through back loop; rep from * to end.

Row 7: K1 through back loop, *P1, K1 through back loop; rep from * to end.

Row 8: Rep row 6.

Rep rows 1–8 for patt.

Woven Horizontal Herringbone

Multiple of 4

Row 1 (RS): K3, *sl 2 wyif, K2; rep from * to last st, K1.

Row 2: P2, *sl 2 wyib, P2; rep from * to last 2 sts, P2.

Row 3: K1, sl 2 wyif, *K2, sl 2 wyif; rep from * to last st, K1.

Row 4: P4, *sl 2 wyib, yf, P2; rep from * to end.

Rows 5–12: Rep rows 1–4 twice.

Row 13: Rep row 3.

Row 14: Rep row 2.

Row 15: Rep row 1.

Row 16: Rep row 4.

Rows 17–24: Rep rows 13–16 twice.

Rep rows 1–24 for patt.

Rickrack Pattern

Multiple of 3 +1

Row 1 (RS): K1 through back loop, *M1, K2tog through back loop, K1 through back loop; rep from * to end.

Row 2: P1 through back loop, *P2, P1 through back loop; rep from * to end.

Row 3: K1 through back loop, *K2tog, M1, K1 through back loop; rep from * to end.

Row 4: Rep row 2.

Rep rows 1–4 for patt.

Garter-Stitch Checks

Multiple of 10 + 5

Row 1 (RS): K5, *P5, K5; rep from * to end.

Row 2: Purl.

Row 3: Rep row 1.

Row 4: Purl.

Rows 5 and 6: Rep row 1.

Row 7: Knit.

Row 8: Rep row 1.

Row 9: Rep row 7.

Row 10: Rep row 1.

Rep rows 1–10 for patt.

Hourglass Eyelets

Multiple of 6 + 1

Row 1 (RS): K6, *P1, K5; rep from * to last st, K1.

Row 2: K1, *P5, K1; rep from * to end.

Row 3: K1, *YO, sl 1, K1, psso, P1, K2tog, YO, K1; rep from * to end.

Row 4: K1, P2, *K1, P5; rep from * to last 4 sts, K1, P2, K1.

Row 5: K3, *P1, K5; rep from * to last 4 sts, P1, K3.

Row 6: Rep row 4.

Row 7: K1, *K2tog, YO, K1, YO, sl 1, K1, psso, P1; rep from * to last 6 sts, K2tog, YO, K1, YO, sl 1, K1, psso, K1.

Row 8: Rep row 2.

Rep rows 1–8 for patt.

Double Rice Stitch

Multiple of 2 + 1

Row 1: P1, *K1 through back loop, P1; rep from * to end.

Row 2 (RS): Knit.

Row 3: *K1 through back loop, P1; rep from * to last st, K1 through back loop.

Row 4: Knit.

Rep rows 1–4 for patt.

Oblong Texture

Multiple of 10 + 1

Row 1 (RS): K3, P5, *K5, P5; rep from * to last 3 sts, K3.

Row 2: P3, K5, *P5, K5; rep from * to last 3 sts, P3.

Row 3: Rep row 2.

Row 4: Rep row 1.

Rep rows 1–4 for patt.

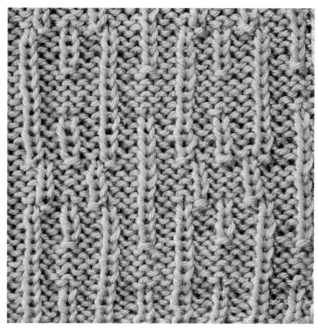

Vertical Dash Stitch

Multiple of 6 + 1

Row 1 (RS): P3, K1, *P5, K1; rep from * to last 3 sts, P3.

Row 2: K3, P1, *K5, P1; rep from * to last 3 sts, K3.

Rows 3 and 4: Rep rows 1 and 2.

Row 5: K1, *P5, K1; rep from * to end.

Row 6: P1, *K5, P1; rep from * to end.

Rows 7 and 8: Rep rows 5 and 6.

Rep rows 1–8 for patt.

Random Dash Pattern

Odd-number multiple of 6 + 1**

Row 1 (RS): K1, *P2, K1; rep from * to end.

Row 2: P1, *K2, P1; rep from * to end.

Rows 3 and 4: Rep rows 1 and 2.

Row 5: K1, *P5, K1; rep from * to end.

Row 6: P1, *K5, P1; rep from * to end.

Rows 7 and 8: Rep rows 5 and 6.

Rows 9 and 11: Rep row 1.

Rows 10 and 12: Rep row 2.

Row 13: P3, *K1, P3; rep from * to end.

Row 14: K3, *P1, K3; rep from * to end.

Rows 15 and 16: Rep rows 13 and 14.

Rep rows 1–16 for patt.

**For example, 6x3, 6x5, 6x7, etc.

Twisted Tree

Worked over 9 sts on a background of reverse St st

Row 1 (RS): P3, K next 3 sts through back loop, P3.

Row 2: K3, P next 3 sts through back loop, K3.

Row 3: P2, twist 2 right, K1 through back loop, twist 2 left, P2.

Row 4: K2, (P1 through back loop, K1) twice, P1 through back loop, K2.

Row 5: P1, twist 2 right, P1, K1 through back loop, P1, twist 2 left, P1.

Row 6: K1, (P1 through back loop, K2) twice, P1 through back loop, K1.

Row 7: Twist 2 right, P1, K next 3 sts through back loop, P1, twist 2 left.

Row 8: P1 through back loop, K2, P next 3 sts through back loop, K2, P1 through back loop.

Rep rows 1–8 for patt.

Waffle Stitch

Multiple of 3 + 1

Row 1 (RS): P1, *K2, P1; rep from * to end.

Row 2: K1, *P2, K1; rep from * to end.

Row 3: Rep row 1.

Row 4: Knit.

Rep rows 1–4 for patt.

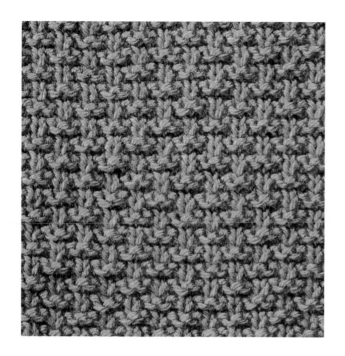

Basket Weave 1

Multiple of 4 + 3

Rows 1 and 3 (RS): Knit.

Row 2: *K3, P1; rep from * to last 3 sts, K3.

Row 4: K1, *P1, K3; rep from * to last 2 sts, P1, K1.

Rep rows 1–4 for patt.

Basket Weave 2

Multiple of 8 + 3

Row 1 (RS): Knit.

Row 2: K4, P3, *K5, P3; rep from * to last 4 sts, K4.

Row 3: P4, K3, *P5, K3; rep from * to last 4 sts, P4.

Row 4: Rep row 2.

Row 5: Knit.

Row 6: P3, *K5, P3; rep from * to end.

Row 7: K3, *P5, K3; rep from * to end.

Row 8: Rep row 6.

Rep rows 1–8 for patt.

Small Basket Stitch

Multiple of 10 + 5

Row 1 (WS): (K1, P1) twice, *K7, P1, K1, P1; rep from * to last st, K1.

Row 2: P1, (K1, P1) twice, *K5, (P1, K1) twice, P1; rep from * to end.

Rows 3 and 4: Rep rows 1 and 2.

Row 5: K6, *P1, K1, P1, K7; rep from * to last 9 sts, P1, K1, P1, K6.

Row 6: *K5, (P1, K1) twice, P1; rep from * to last 5 sts, K5.

Rows 7 and 8: Rep rows 5 and 6.

Rep rows 1–8 for patt.

Wavy Rib

Multiple of 6 + 2

Row 1 (RS): P2, *K4, P2; rep from * to end.

Row 2: K2, *P4, K2; rep from * to end.

Rows 3 and 4: Rep rows 1 and 2.

Row 5: K3, P2, *K4, P2; rep from * to last 3 sts, K3.

Row 6: P3, K2, *P4, K2; rep from * to last 3 sts, P3.

Rows 7 and 8: Rep rows 5 and 6.

Rep rows 1–8 for patt.

Diagonal Garter Ribs

Multiple of 5 + 2

Row 1 and all odd rows (RS): Knit.

Row 2: *P2, K3; rep from * to last 2 sts, P2.

Row 4: K1, *P2, K3; rep from * to last st, P1.

Row 6: K2, *P2, K3; rep from * to end.

Row 8: *K3, P2; rep from * to last 2 sts, K2.

Row 10: P1, *K3, P2; rep from * to last st, K1.

Rep rows 1–10 for patt.

Tweed Stitch

Multiple of 2 + 1

Row 1 (RS): K1, *sl 1 wyif, K1; rep from * to end.

Row 2: P2, *sl 1 wyib, P1; rep from * to last st, P1.

Rep rows 1 and 2 for patt.

Woven Stitch 2

Multiple of 2 + 1

Row 1 (RS): K1, *sl 1 wyif, K1; rep from * to end.

Row 2: Purl.

Row 3: K2, *sl 1 wyif, K1; rep from * to last st, K1.

Row 4: Purl.

Rep rows 1–4 for patt.

Knot Stitch

Multiple of 2 + 1

Row 1 (RS): Knit.

Row 2: K1, *P2tog without slipping sts off needle, then knit tog the same 2 sts; rep from * to end.

Row 3: Knit.

Row 4: *P2tog without slipping sts off needle, then knit tog the same 2 sts; rep from * to last st, K1.

Rep these 4 rows.

Seed Stitch 2

Multiple of 4 + 3

Row 1 (RS): P1, K1, *P3, K1; rep from * to last st, P1.

Row 2: K3, *P1, K3; rep from * to end.

Rep rows 1 and 2 for patt.

Seed Stitch 3

Multiple of 4 + 3

Row 1: P1, K1, *P3, K1; rep from * to last st, P1.

Row 2 (RS): K3, *P1, K3; rep from * to end.

Rep rows 1 and 2 for patt.

Double Seed Stitch

Multiple of 5 + 2

Row 1 (RS): K2, *P3, K2; rep from * to end.

Row 2: Purl.

Row 3: *P3, K2; rep to last 2 sts, P2.

Row 4: Purl.

Rep rows 1–4 for patt.

Andalusian Stitch

Multiple of 2

Row 1 (RS): Knit.

Row 2: Purl.

Row 3: *K1, P1; rep from * to end.

Row 4: Purl.

Rep rows 1–4 for patt.

Double Andalusian Stitch

Multiple of 6

Row 1 (RS): Knit.

Row 2: *K2, P4; rep from * to end.

Row 3: Knit.

Row 4: P3, *K2, P4; rep from * to last 3 sts; K2, P1.

Row 5: Knit.

Rep rows 2–5 for patt.

Seed-Stitch Checks

Multiple of 10 + 5

Row 1 (RS): K5, *(P1, K1) twice, P1, K5; rep from * to end.

Row 2: P6, *K1, P1, K1, P7; rep from * to last 9 sts, K1, P1, K1, P6.

Rows 3 and 4: Rep rows 1 and 2.

Row 5: Rep row 1.

Row 6: *(K1, P1) twice, K1, P5; rep from * to last 5 sts, (K1, P1) twice, K1.

Row 7: (K1, P1) twice, *K7, P1, K1, P1; rep from * to last st, K1.

Rows 8 and 9: Rep rows 6 and 7.

Row 10: Rep row 6.

Rep rows 1–10 for patt.

Double Signal Check

Multiple of 18 + 9

Row 1 (RS): K1, P7, K1, *P1, K7, P1, K1, P7, K1; rep from * to end.

Row 2: P2, K5, P2, *K2, P5, K2, P2, K5, P2; rep from * to end.

Row 3: K3, *P3, K3; rep from * to end.

Row 4: P4, K1, P4, *K4, P1, K4, P4, K1, P4; rep from * to end.

Row 5: P1, K7, P1, *K1, P7, K1, P1, K7, P1; rep from * to end.

Row 6: K2, P5, K2, *P2, K5, P2, K2, P5, K2; rep from * to end.

Row 7: P3, *K3, P3; rep from * to end.

Row 8: K4, P1, K4, *P4, K1, P4, K4, P1, K4; rep from * to end.

Rep rows 1–8 for patt.

Moss-Stitch Diamonds

Multiple of 10 + 9

Row 1 (RS): K4, *P1, K9; rep from * to last 5 sts, P1, K4.

Row 2: P3, *K1, P1, K1, P7; rep from * to last 6 sts, K1, P1, K1, P3.

Row 3: K2, *(P1, K1) twice, P1, K5; rep from * to last 7 sts, (P1, K1) twice, P1, K2.

Row 4: (P1, K1) 4 times, *P3, (K1, P1) 3 times, K1; rep from * to last st, P1.

Row 5: P1, *K1, P1; rep from * to end.

Row 6: Rep row 4.

Row 7: Rep row 3.

Row 8: Rep row 2.

Row 9: Rep row 1.

Row 10: Purl.

Rep rows 1–10 for patt.

Zigzag Moss Stitch

Multiple of 6 + 1

Row 1 (RS): Knit.

Row 2: Purl.

Row 3: P1, *K5, P1; rep from * to end.

Row 4: P1, *K1, P3, K1, P1; rep from * to end.

Rows 5 and 6: P1, *K1, P1; rep from * to end.

Row 7: K2, P1, K1, P1, *K3, P1, K1, P1; rep from * to last 2 sts, K2.

Row 8: P3, K1, *P5, K1; rep from * to last 3 sts, P3.

Row 9: Knit.

Row 10: Purl.

Row 11: K3, *P1, K5; rep from * to last 4 sts, P1, K3.

Row 12: P2, *K1, P1, K1, P3; rep from * to last 5 sts; K1, P1, K1, P2.

Rows 13 and 14: K1, *P1, K1; rep from * to end.

Row 15: K1, P1, *K3, P1, K1, P1; rep from * to last 5 sts, K3, P1, K1.

Row 16: K1, *P5, K1; rep from * to end.

Rep rows 1–16 for patt.

Garter-Stitch Ridges

Any number of stitches

Row 1 (RS): Knit.

Row 2: Purl.

Row 3: Knit.

Rows 4–10: Purl.

Rep rows 1–10 for patt.

Triangle Rib

Multiple of 8

Row 1 (RS): *P2, K6; rep from * to end.

Row 2: *P6, K2; rep from * to end.

Row 3: *P3, K5; rep from * to end.

Row 4: *P4, K4; rep from * to end.

Row 5: *P5, K3; rep from * to end.

Row 6: *P2, K6; rep from * to end.

Row 7: *P7, K1; rep from * to end.

Row 8: *P2, K6; rep from * to end.

Row 9: Rep row 5.

Row 10: Rep row 4.

Row 11: Rep row 3.

Row 12: Rep row 2.

Rep rows 1–12 for patt.

Moss-Stitch Triangles

Multiple of 8

Row 1 (RS): *P1, K7; rep from * to end.

Row 2: P6, *K1, P7; rep from * to last 2 sts, K1, P1.

Row 3: *P1, K1, P1, K5; rep from * to end.

Row 4: P4, *K1, P1, K1, P5; rep from * to last 4 sts, (K1, P1) twice.

Row 5: *(P1, K1) twice, P1, K3; rep from * to end.

Row 6: P2, *(K1, P1) twice, K1, P3; rep from * to last 6 sts, (K1, P1) 3 times.

Row 7: *P1, K1; rep from * to end.

Row 8: Rep row 6.

Row 9: Rep row 5.

Row 10: Rep row 4.

Row 11: Rep row 3.

Row 12: Rep row 2.

Rep rows 1–12 for patt.

Moss-Stitch Panes

Multiple of 10 + 3

Row 1 (RS): P1, *K1, P1; rep from * to end.

Row 2: P1, *K1, P1; rep from * to end.

Row 3: P1, K1, P1, *K7, P1, K1, P1; rep from * to end.

Row 4: P1, K1, P9, *K1, P9; rep from * to last 2 sts, K1, P1.

Rows 5–10: Rep rows 3 and 4 three more times.

Rep rows 1–10 for patt.

Chevron Stripes

Multiple of 18 + 9

Row 1 (RS): P4, K1, P4, *K4, P1, K4, P4, K1, P4; rep from * to end.

Row 2: K3, *P3, K3; rep from * to end.

Row 3: P2, K5, P2, *K2, P5, K2, P2, K5, P2; rep from * to end.

Row 4: K1, P7, K1, *P1, K7, P1, K1, P7, K1; rep from * to end.

Row 5: K4, P1, K4, *P4, K1, P4, K4, P1, K4; rep from * to end.

Row 6: P3, *K3, P3; rep from * to end.

Row 7: K2, P5, K2, *P2, K5, P2, K2, P5, K2; rep from * to end.

Row 8: P1, K7, P1, *K1, P7, K1, P1, K7, P1; rep from * to end.

Rep rows 1–8 for patt.

Plain Diamonds

Multiple of 9

Row 1 (RS): K4, *P1, K8; rep from * to last 5 sts, P1, K4.

Row 2: P3, *K3, P6; rep from * to last 6 sts, K3, P3.

Row 3: K2, *P5, K4; rep from * to last 7 sts, P5, K2.

Row 4: P1, *K7, P2; rep from * to last 8 sts, K7, P1.

Row 5: Purl.

Row 6: Rep row 4.

Row 7: Rep row 3.

Row 8: Rep row 2.

Rep rows 1–8 for patt.

Moss-Stitch Parallelograms

Multiple of 10

Row 1 (RS): *K5, (P1, K1) twice, P1; rep from * to end.

Row 2: (P1, K1) 3 times, *P5, (K1, P1) twice, K1; rep from * to last 4 sts, P4.

Row 3: K3, *(P1, K1) twice, P1, K5; rep from * to last 7 sts, (P1, K1) twice, P1, K2.

Row 4: P3, *(K1, P1) twice, K1, P5; rep from * to last 7 sts, (K1, P1) twice, K1, P2.

Row 5: (K1, P1) 3 times, *K5, (P1, K1) twice, P1; rep from * to last 4 sts, K4.

Row 6: Purl.

Rep rows 1–6 for patt.

Ripple Pattern

Multiple of 8 + 6

Row 1 (RS): K6, *P2, K6; rep from * to end.

Row 2: K1, *P4, K4; rep from * to last 5 sts, P4, K1.

Row 3: P2, *K2, P2; rep from * to end.

Row 4: P1, *K4, P4; rep from * to last 5 sts, K4, P1.

Row 5: K2, *P2, K6; rep from * to last 4 sts, P2, K2.

Row 6: P6, *K2, P6; rep from * to end.

Row 7: Rep row 4.

Row 8: K2, *P2, K2; rep from * to end.

Row 9: Rep row 2.

Row 10: P2, *K2, P6; rep from * to last 4 sts, K2, P2.

Rep rows 1–10 for patt.

Parallelogram Check

Multiple of 10

Row 1 (RS): *K5, P5; rep from * to end.

Row 2: K4, *P5, K5; rep from * to last 6 sts, P5, K1.

Row 3: P2, *K5, P5; rep from * to last 8 sts, K5, P3.

Row 4: K2, *P5, K5; rep from * to last 8 sts, P5, K3.

Row 5: P4, *K5, P5; rep from * to last 6 sts, K5, P1.

Row 6: *P5, K5; rep from * to end.

Rep rows 1–6 for patt.

Moss-Stitch Diagonal

Multiple of 8 + 3

Row 1 (RS): K4, *P1, K1, P1, K5; rep from * to last 7 sts, P1, K1, P1, K4.

Row 2: P3, *(K1, P1) twice, K1, P3; rep from * to end.

Row 3: K2, *P1, K1, P1, K5; rep from * to last st, P1.

Row 4: P1, K1, *P3, (K1, P1) twice, K1; rep from * to last st, P1.

Row 5: *P1, K1, P1, K5; rep from * to last 3 sts, P1, K1, P1.

Row 6: *(P1, K1) twice, P3, K1; rep from * to last 3 sts, P1, K1, P1.

Row 7: P1, *K5, P1, K1, P1; rep from * to last 2 sts, K2.

Row 8: (P1, K1) 3 times, *P3, (K1, P1) twice, K1; rep from * to last 5 sts, P3, K1, P1.

Rep rows 1–8 for patt.

Zigzag Stitch

Multiple of 6

Row 1 (RS): *K3, P3; rep from * to end.

Row 2 and all even rows: Purl.

Row 3: P1, *K3, P3; rep from * to last 5 sts, K3, P2.

Row 5: P2, *K3, P3; rep from * to last 4 sts, K3, P1.

Row 7: *P3, K3; rep from * to end.

Row 9: Rep row 5.

Row 11: Rep row 3.

Row 12: Purl.

Rep rows 1–12 for patt.

Mock Cable on Moss Stitch

Multiple of 9 + 5

Row 1 (WS): (K1, P1) twice, K1, *K1 through back loop, P2, K1 through back loop, (K1, P1) twice, K1; rep from * to end.

Row 2: *(K1, P1) 3 times, K2, P1; rep from * to last 5 sts, (K1, P1) twice, K1.

Rows 3 and 4: Rep rows 1 and 2.

Row 5: (K1, P1) twice, K1, *YO, K1, P2, K1, lift YO over last 4 sts and off needle, (K1, P1) twice, K1; rep from * to end.

Row 6: Rep row 2.

Rep rows 1–6 for patt.

Twisted Check

Multiple of 4 + 2

Row 1 (RS): Knit all sts through back loops.

Row 2: Purl.

Row 3: Knit next 2 sts through back loop, *P2, K2 sts; rep from * to end.

Row 4: P2, *K2, P2; rep from * to end.

Rows 5 and 6: Rep rows 1 and 2.

Row 7: P2, *K next 2 sts through back loop, P2; rep from * to end.

Row 8: K2, *P2, K2; rep from * to end.

Rep rows 1–8 for patt.

Rose Stitch

Multiple of 2 + 1

Row 1: K2, *P1, K1; rep from * to last st, K1.

Row 2 (RS): K1, *K1 in st below, K1; rep from * to end.

Row 3: K1, *P1, K1; rep from * to end.

Row 4: K2, *K1 in st below, K1; rep from * to last st, K1.

Rep rows 1–4 for patt.

Half Brioche Stitch

Multiple of 2 + 1

Row 1: Purl.

Row 2 (RS): K1, *K1 in st below, K1; rep from * to end.

Row 3: Purl.

Row 4: K1 in st below, *K1, K1 in st below; rep from * to end.

Rep rows 1–4 for patt.

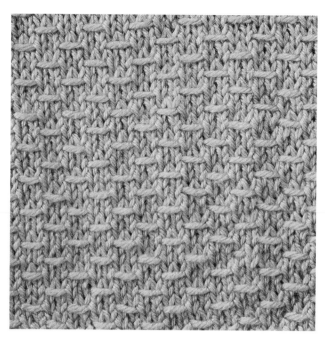

Diamond Drops

Multiple of 4

Row 1 (RS): Knit.

Row 2: P1, *YO, P2, pass YO over purl sts, P2; rep from * to last 3 sts, YO, P2, pass YO over purl sts, P1.

Row 3: Knit.

Row 4: P3, *YO, P2, pass YO over purl sts, P2; rep from * to last st, P1.

Rep rows 1–4 for patt.

Double Woven Stitch

Multiple of 4

Row 1 (RS): K3, *sl 2 wyif, K2; rep from * to last st, K1.

Row 2: Purl.

Row 3: K1, *sl 2 wyif, K2; rep from * to last 3 sts, sl 2 wyif, K1.

Row 4: Purl.

Rep rows 1–4 for patt.

Herringbone

Multiple of 7 + 1

Row 1: Purl.

Row 2 (RS): *K2tog, K2, K1 through back loop of st below, then knit st above, K2; rep from * to last st, K1.

Row 3: Purl.

Row 4: K3, K1 through back loop of st below, then knit st above, K2, K2tog, *K2, K1 through back loop of st below, then knit st above, K2, K2tog; rep from * to end.

Rep rows 1–4 for patt.

Horizontal Herringbone

Multiple of 2

Row 1 (RS): K1, *sl 1, K1, psso but instead of dropping slipped st from left-hand needle, knit into back of it; rep from * to last st, K1.

Row 2: *P2tog, then purl first st again, slipping both sts off needle tog; rep from * to end.

Rep rows 1 and 2 for patt.

Diagonal Rib 2

Multiple of 4

Rows 1 and 2: *K2, P2; rep from * to end.

Row 3 (RS): K1, *P2, K2; rep from * to last 3 sts, P2, K1.

Row 4: P1, *K2, P2; rep from * to last 3 sts, K2, P1.

Rows 5 and 6: *P2, K2; rep from * to end.

Row 7: Rep row 4.

Row 8: Rep row 3.

Rep rows 1–8 for patt.

Mock-Rib Checks

Multiple of 2

Row 1 (RS): Purl.

Row 2: *K1, K1 in st below; rep from * to last 2 sts, K2.

Rows 3–7: Rep row 2 five more times.

Row 8: K2, *K1 in st below, K1; rep from * to end.

Rows 9–13: Rep row 8 five more times.

Rep rows 2–13 for patt.

Star-Stitch Pattern

Multiple of 4 + 1

Row 1 (RS): P1, *K1, P1; rep from * to end.

Row 2: K1, *MS, K1; rep from * to end.

Row 3: Rep row 1.

Row 4: K1, P1, K1, *MS, K1; rep from * to last 2 sts, P1, K1.

Rep rows 1–4 for patt.

Blanket Moss Stitch

Multiple of 2 + 1

Note: St count changes from row to row; count sts after the 2nd and 4th rows of patt for original st count.

Row 1 (RS): Knit into front and back of each st (thus doubling the number of sts).

Row 2: K2tog, *P2tog, K2tog; rep from * to end (original number of sts restored).

Row 3: Rep row 1.

Row 4: P2tog, *K2tog, P2tog; rep from * to end.

Rep rows 1–4 for patt.

Lizard Lattice

Multiple of 6 + 3

Row 1 (RS): Knit.

Row 2: Purl.

Rows 3 and 4: Rep rows 1 and 2.

Row 5: P3, *K3, P3; rep from * to end.

Row 6: Purl.

Rows 7–9: Rep rows 5 and 6, then rep row 5 again.

Row 10: Purl.

Row 11: Knit.

Rows 12 and 13: Rep rows 10 and 11.

Row 14: P3, *K3, P3; rep from * to end.

Row 15: Knit.

Rows 16–18: Rep rows 14 and 15, then rep row 14 again.

Rep rows 1–18 for patt.

Spiral Pattern

Multiple of 7

Row 1 (RS): P2, K4, *P3, K4; rep from * to last st, P1.

Row 2: K1, P3, *K4, P3; rep from * to last 3 sts, K3.

Row 3: P1, K1, P2, *K2, P2, K1, P2; rep from * to last 3 sts, K2, P1.

Row 4: K1, P1, K2, P2, *K2, P1, K2, P2; rep from * to last st, K1.

Row 5: P1, K3, *P4, K3; rep from * to last 3 sts, P3.

Row 6: K2, P4, *K3, P4; rep from * to last st, K1.

Row 7: P1, K5, *P2, K5; rep from * to last st, P1.

Row 8: K1, P5, *K2, P5; rep from * to last st, K1.

Rep rows 1–8 for patt.

Staggered Brioche Rib

Multiple of 2 + 1

Row 1: Knit.

Row 2 (RS): K1, *K1 in st below, K1; rep from * to end.

Rows 3–5: Rep row 2 three more times.

Row 6: K2, K1 in st below, *K1, K1 in st below; rep from * to last 2 sts, K2.

Rows 7–9: Rep row 6 three more times.

Rep rows 2–9 for patt.

Seed-Pearl Grid

Multiple of 8 + 1

Row 1 and all odd rows: Purl.

Row 2 (RS): P1, *K1, P1; rep from * to end.

Row 4: Knit.

Row 6: P1, *K7, P1; rep from * to end.

Row 8: Knit.

Row 10: Rep row 6.

Row 12: Knit.

Rep rows 1–12 for patt.

Simple Seed Stitch

Multiple of 4 + 1

Row 1 (RS): P1, *K3, P1; rep from * to end.

Row 2 and all even rows: Purl.

Row 3: Knit.

Row 5: K2, P1, *K3, P1; rep from * to last 2 sts, K2.

Row 7: Knit.

Row 8: Purl.

Rep rows 1–8 for patt.

Broken Chevron

Multiple of 12

Row 1 (RS): K1, P2, *K2, P2; rep from * to last st, K1.

Row 2: P1, K2, *P2, K2; rep from * to last st, P1.

Row 3: *P4, K2; rep from * to end.

Row 4: *P2, K4; rep from * to end.

Row 5: Rep row 2.

Row 6: K1, P2, *K2, P2; rep from * to last st, K1.

Row 7: *K2, P6, K2, P2; rep from * to end.

Row 8: *K2, P2, K6, P2; rep from * to end.

Rows 9–14: Rep rows 1–6.

Row 15: (P2, K2) twice, *P6, K2, P2, K2; rep from * to last 4 sts, P4.

Row 16: K4, P2, K2, P2, *K6, P2, K2, P2; rep from * to last 2 sts, K2.

Rep rows 1–16 for patt.

Moss-Stitch Zigzag

Multiple of 9

Row 1 (RS): *(K1, P1) twice, K4, P1; rep from * to end.

Row 2: *P4, (K1, P1) twice, K1; rep from * to end.

Row 3: (K1, P1) 3 times, *K4, (P1, K1) twice, P1; rep from * to last 3 sts, K3.

Row 4: P2, *(K1, P1) twice, K1, P4; rep from * to last 7 sts, (K1, P1) twice, K1, P2.

Row 5: K3, *(P1, K1) twice, P1, K4; rep from * to last 6 sts, (P1, K1) 3 times.

Row 6: *(K1, P1) twice, K1, P4; rep from * to end.

Row 7: Rep row 5.

Row 8: Rep row 4.

Row 9: Rep row 3.

Row 10: Rep row 2.

Rep rows 1–10 for patt.

Moss Slip Stitch

Multiple of 2 + 1

Row 1 (RS): K1, *sl 1, K1; rep from * to end.

Row 2: K1, *sl 1 wyif, K1; rep from * to end.

Row 3: K2, *sl 1, K1; rep from * to last st, K1.

Row 4: K2, *sl 1 wyif, K1; rep from * to last st, K1.

Rep rows 1–4 for patt.

Twisted Moss

Multiple of 2 + 1

Row 1: Knit.

Row 2 (RS): K1, *K1 in st below, K1; rep from * to end.

Row 3: Knit.

Row 4: K1 in st below, *K1, K1 in st below; rep from * to end.

Rep rows 1–4 for patt.

Embossed Diamonds

Multiple of 10 + 3

Row 1 (RS): P1, K1, P1, *(K3, P1) twice, K1, P1; rep from * to end.

Row 2: P1, K1, *P3, K1, P1, K1, P3, K1; rep from * to last st, P1.

Row 3: K4, *(P1, K1) twice, P1, K5; rep from * to last 9 sts, (P1, K1) twice, P1, K4.

Row 4: P3, *(K1, P1) 3 times, K1, P3; rep from * to end.

Row 5: Rep row 3.

Row 6: Rep row 2.

Row 7: Rep row 1.

Row 8: P1, K1, P1, *K1, P5, (K1, P1) twice; rep from * to end.

Row 9: (P1, K1) twice, *P1, K3, (P1, K1) 3 times; rep from * to last 9 sts, P1, K3, (P1, K1) twice, P1.

Row 10: Rep row 8.

Rep rows 1–10 for patt.

Diamond Brocade

Multiple of 8 + 1

Row 1 (RS): K4, *P1, K7; rep from * to last 5 sts, P1, K4.

Row 2: P3, *K1, P1, K1, P5; rep from * to last 6 sts, K1, P1, K1, P3.

Row 3: K2, *P1, K3; rep from * to last 3 sts, P1, K2.

Row 4: P1, *K1, P5, K1, P1, rep from * to end.

Row 5: *P1, K7; rep from * to last st, P1.

Row 6: Rep row 4.

Row 7: Rep row 3.

Row 8: Rep row 2.

Rep rows 1–8 for patt.

King Charles Brocade

Multiple of 12 + 1

Row 1 (RS): K1, *P1, K9, P1, K1; rep from * to end.

Row 2: K1, P1, K1, *P7, (K1, P1) twice, K1; rep from * to last 10 sts, P7, K1, P1, K1.

Row 3: (K1, P1) twice, *K5, (P1, K1) 3 times, P1; rep from * to last 9 sts, K5, (P1, K1) twice.

Row 4: P2, *K1, P1, K1, P3; rep from * to last 5 sts, K1, P1, K1, P2.

Row 5: K3, *(P1, K1) 3 times, P1, K5; rep from * to last 10 sts, (P1, K1) 3 times, P1, K3.

Row 6: P4, *(K1, P1) twice, K1, P7; rep from * to last 9 sts, (K1, P1) twice, K1, P4.

Row 7: K5, *P1, K1, P1, K9; rep from * to last 8 sts, P1, K1, P1, K5.

Row 8: Rep row 6.

Row 9: Rep row 5.

Row 10: Rep row 4.

Row 11: Rep row 3.

Row 12: Rep row 2.

Rep rows 1–12 for patt.

Inverness Diamond

Multiple of 17

Row 1: P1, K3, P9, K3, *P2, K3, P9, K3; rep from * to last st, P1.

Row 2 (RS): K2, P3, K7, P3, *K4, P3, K7, P3; rep from * to last 2 sts, K2.

Row 3: P3, K3, P5, K3, *P6, K3, P5, K3; rep from * to last 3 sts, P3.

Row 4: K4, P3, K3, P3, *K8, P3, K3, P3; rep from * to last 4 sts, K4.

Row 5: P5, K3, P1, K3, *P10, K3, P1, K3; rep from * to last 5 sts, P5.

Row 6: K6, P5, *K12, P5; rep from * to last 6 sts, K6.

Row 7: P7, K3, *P14, K3; rep from * to last 7 sts, P7.

Row 8: K6, P5, *K12, P5; rep from * to last 6 sts, K6.

Row 9: Rep row 5.

Row 10: Rep row 4.

Row 11: Rep row 3.

Row 12: Rep row 2.

Rep rows 1–12 for patt.

Loop Pattern

Multiple of 2

Row 1 (RS): Knit.

Row 2: * K1, sl 1; rep from * to last 2 sts, K2.

Row 3: Knit.

Row 4: K2, *sl 1, K1; rep from * to end.

Rep rows 1–4 for patt.

Hindu Pillar Stitch

Multiple of 4 + 1

Row 1 (RS): K1, *P3tog without slipping sts
from left-hand needle, knit them tog, then
purl them tog, K1; rep from * to end.

Row 2: Purl.

Rep rows 1 and 2 for patt.

Bee Stitch

Multiple of 2 + 1

Row 1: Knit.

Row 2 (RS): K1, *K1 in st below, K1; rep from *
to end.

Row 3: Knit.

Row 4: K2, K1 in st below, *K1, K1 in st below;
rep from * to last 2 sts, K2.

Rep rows 1–4 for patt.

Elongated Chevron

Multiple of 18 + 1

Row 1 (RS): P1, *(K2, P2) twice, K1, (P2, K2) twice, P1; rep from * to end.

Row 2: K1, *(P2, K2) twice, P1, (K2, P2) twice, K1; rep from * to end.

Row 3: Rep row 1.

Row 4: Rep row 2.

Row 5: (P2, K2) twice, *P3, K2, P2, K2; rep from * to last 2 sts, P2.

Row 6: (K2, P2) twice, *K3, P2, K2, P2; rep from * to last 2 sts, K2.

Row 7: Rep row 5.

Row 8: Rep row 6.

Row 9: Rep row 2.

Rows 10 and 11: Rep rows 1 and 2.

Row 12: Rep row 1.

Row 13: Rep row 6.

Rows 14 and 15: Rep rows 5 and 6.

Row 16: Rep row 5.

Rep rows 1–16 for patt.

Reverse Stockinette Chevron

Multiple of 6 + 5

Row 1 (RS): K5, *P1, K5; rep from * to end.

Row 2: K1, *P3, K3; rep from * to last 4 sts, P3, K1.

Row 3: P2, *K1, P2; rep from * to end.

Row 4: P1, *K3, P3; rep from * to last 4 sts, K3, P1.

Row 5: K2, *P1, K5; rep from * to last 3 sts, P1, K2.

Row 6: Purl.

Rep rows 1–6 for patt.

Rice Stitch

Multiple of 2 + 1

Row 1 (RS): P1, *K1 through back loop, P1; rep from * to end.

Row 2: Knit.

Rep rows 1 and 2 for patt.

Textured Strip

Multiple of 3

Row 1 (RS): Knit.

Row 2: Purl.

Row 3: Knit.

Row 4: Purl.

Row 5: K1, *P1, K2; rep from * to last 2 sts, P1, K1.

Row 6: P1, *K1, P2; rep from * to last 2 sts, K1, P1.

Rows 7 and 8: Rep rows 5 and 6.

Row 9: *P2, K1; rep from * to end.

Row 10: *P1, K2; rep from * to end.

Rows 11 and 12: Rep rows 9 and 10.

Rep rows 1–12 for patt.

Goblets

Multiple of 6 + 2

Row 1 (RS): P3, K2, *P4, K2; rep from * to last 3 sts, P3.

Row 2: K3, P2, *K4, P2; rep from * to last 3 sts, K3.

Rows 3 and 4: Rep rows 1 and 2.

Row 5: P2, *K4, P2; rep from * to end.

Row 6: K2, *P4, K2; rep from * to end.

Rows 7 and 8: Rep rows 5 and 6.

Row 9: Purl.

Row 10: Knit.

Rep rows 1–10 for patt.

Bamboo Stitch

Multiple of 2

Row 1: *YO, K2, pass YO over K2; rep from * to end.

Row 2: Purl.

Rep rows 1 and 2 for patt.

Basket Rib

Multiple of 2 + 1

Row 1 (RS): Knit.

Row 2: Purl.

Row 3: K1, *sl 1 wyib, K1; rep from * to end.

Row 4: K1, *sl 1 wyif, K1; rep from * to end.

Rep rows 1–4 for patt.

Brick Rib

Multiple of 3 + 1

Row 1 (RS): *P2, K next st through back loop; rep from * to last st, P1.

Row 2: K1, *P next st through back loop, K2; rep from * to end.

Rows 3 and 4: Rep rows 1 and 2.

Row 5: P1, *, K next 2 sts through back loop, P1; rep from * to end.

Row 6: K1, *P next 2 sts through back loop, K1; rep from * to end.

Rows 7 and 8: Rep rows 5 and 6.

Row 9: P1, *K next st through back loop, P2; rep from * to end.

Row 10: *K2, P next st through back loop; rep from * to last st, K1.

Rows 11 and 12: Rep rows 9 and 10.

Rep rows 1–12 for patt.

Lacy Rib

Multiple of 3 + 1

Row 1 (RS): K1, *K2tog, YO, P1; rep from * to last 3 sts, K2tog, YO, K1.

Row 2: P3, *K1, P2; rep from * to last 4 sts, K1, P3.

Row 3: K1, YO, sl 1, K1, psso, *P1, YO, sl 1, K1, psso; rep from * to last st, K1.

Row 4: Rep row 2.

Rep rows 1–4 for patt.

Simple Lace Rib

Multiple of 6 + 1

Row 1 (RS): Knit next 2 sts through back loop, *K3, knit next 3 sts through back loop; rep from * to last 5 sts, K3, knit next 2 sts through back loop.

Row 2: Purl first 2 sts through back loop, *P3, purl next 3 sts through back loop; rep from * to last 5 sts, P3, purl next 2 sts through

gh back loop,
D, knit next 3 sts
om * to last 5 sts,
knit next 2 sts

Herringbone Lace Rib

Multiple of 7 + 1

Row 1 (RS): K1, *P1, K1, YO, P2tog, K1, P1, K1; rep from * to end.

Row 2: P1, *K2, YO, P2tog, K2, P1; rep from * to end.

Rep rows 1 and 2 for patt.

Eyelets

Multiple of 3 + 2

Row 1 (RS): Knit.

Row 2: Purl.

Row 3: K2, *YO, K2tog, K1; rep from * to end.

Row 4: Purl.

Rep rows 1–4 for patt.

Garter Stitch Twisted Rib

Multiple of 4

Row 1 (RS): K1, *cross 2 back, K2; rep from * to last 3 sts, cross 2 back, K1.

Row 2: K1, *yf, cross 2 purl, yb, K2; rep from * to last 3 sts, yf, cross 2 purl, yb, K1.

Rep rows 1 and 2 for patt.

Contrary Fisherman's Rib

Multiple of 2 + 1

Foundation row: Knit.

Row 1 (RS): Sl 1, *K1 in st below, K1; rep from * to end.

Row 2: Sl 1, *K1, K1 in st below; rep from * to last 2 sts, K2.

Rows 3 and 4: Rep rows 1 and 2.

Row 5: Rep row 1.

Row 6: Sl 1, *K1 in st below, K1; rep from * to end.

Row 7: Rep row 2.

Row 8: Rep row 6.

Row 9: Rep row 2.

Row 10: Rep row 6.

Rep rows 1–10 for patt.

Tweed Mock Rib

Multiple of 2

Row 1: K1, *sl 1 purlwise, K1, YO, psso the K1 and YO; rep from * to last st, K1.

Row 2: Purl.

Rep rows 1 and 2 for patt.

Loop Stitch Rib

Multiple of 8 + 4

Row 1 (RS): *P4, K4 elongated sts (knit st, wrapping the yarn 3 times around the right-hand needle); rep from * to last 4 sts, P4.

Row 2: K4, *wyif, sl the 4 long sts purlwise, letting extra loops drop, K4; rep from * to end.

Row 3: *P4, sl 4 wyib, yf; rep from * to end, P4.

Row 4: Rep row 2.

Row 5: Rep row 1.

Rep rows 2–5 for patt.

Broken Rib

Multiple of 2 + 1

Row 1 (RS): Knit.

Row 2: P1, *K1, P1; rep from * to end.

Rep rows 1 and 2 for patt.

Diagonal Rib 1

Multiple of 4

Row 1 (RS): *K2, P2; rep from * to end.

Row 2: Rep row 1.

Row 3: K1, *P2, K2; rep from * to last 3 sts, P2, K1.

Row 4: P1, *K2, P2; rep from * to last 3 sts, K2, P1.

Row 5: *P2, K2; rep from * to end.

Row 6: Rep row 5.

Row 7: Rep row 4.

Row 8: Rep row 3.

Rep rows 1–8 for patt.

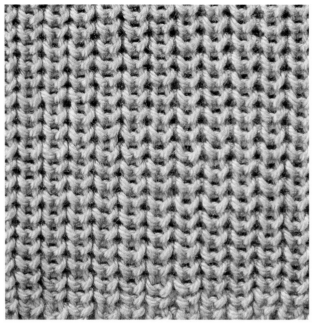

Fisherman's Rib

Even number of sts

Row 1: Purl.

Row 2 (RS): *P1, K1 in st below; rep from * to
last 2 sts, P2.

Rep row 2 for patt.

Half Fisherman's Rib

Multiple of 2 + 1

Row 1 (RS): Sl 1, knit to end.

Row 2: Sl 1, *K1 in st below, P1; rep from * to
end.

Rep rows 1 and 2 for patt.

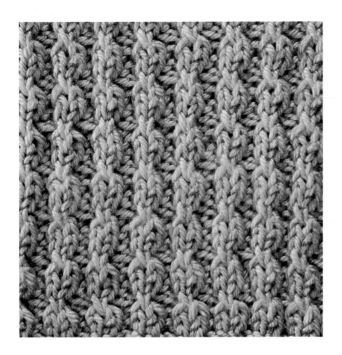

Little Hourglass Rib

Multiple of 4 + 2

Row 1: K2, *P2, K2; rep from * to end.

Row 2 (RS): P2, *K2tog through back loops, then knit same 2 sts tog through front loops, P2; rep from * to end.

Row 3: K2, *P1, YO, P1, K2; rep from * to end.

Row 4: P2, *sl 1 wyib, K1, psso, K1, P2; rep from * to end.

Rep rows 1–4 for patt.

Ridged Rib

Multiple of 2 + 1

Rows 1 and 2: Knit.

Row 3 (RS): P1, *K1, P1; rep from * to end.

Row 4: K1, *P1, K1; rep from * to end.

Rep rows 1–4 for patt.

Double-Ridged Rib

Multiple of 2 + 1

Rows 1 and 2: Knit.

Row 3 (RS): P1, *K1, P1; rep from * to end.

Row 4: K1, *P1, K1; rep from * to end.

Rows 5 and 6: Knit.

Row 7: Rep row 4.

Row 8: P1, *K1, P1; rep from * to end.

Rep rows 1–8 for patt.

Interrupted Rib

Multiple of 2 + 1

Row 1 (RS): P1, *K1, P1; rep from * to end.

Row 2: K1, *P1, K1; rep from * to end.

Row 3: Purl.

Row 4: Knit.

Rep rows 1–4 for patt.

Slip-Stitch Rib

Multiple of 2 + 1

Row 1: Purl.

Row 2 (RS): K1, *sl 1 wyif, K1; rep from * to end.

Rep rows 1 and 2 for patt.

Granite Rib

Multiple of 8 + 2

Row 1 (RS): K2, *(cross 2 front) 3 times, K2; rep from * to end.

Row 2: Purl.

Row 3: K2, *(knit third st from left-hand needle, then second st, then first st, slipping all 3 sts off needle tog) twice, K2; rep from * to end.

Row 4: Purl.

Rep rows 1–4 for patt.

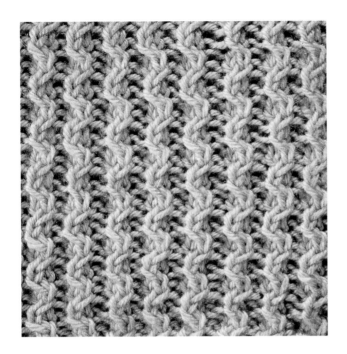

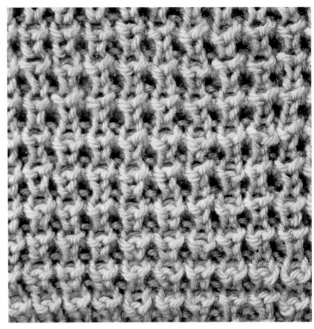

Ripple Rib

Multiple of 3 + 1

Row 1: K1, *P2, K1; rep from * to end.

Row 2 (RS): P1, *cross 2 front, P1; rep from * to end.

Row 3: Rep row 1.

Row 4: P1, *cross 2 back, P1; rep from * to end.

Rep rows 1–4 for patt.

Square Rib

Multiple of 2 + 1

Row 1 (RS): K2, P1, *K1, P1; rep from * to last 2 sts, K2.

Row 2: K1, *P1, K1; rep from * to end.

Row 3: Rep row 1.

Row 4: K1, P1, *yb, insert needle through center of st 2 rows below next st on needle and knit this in the usual way, slipping st above it off needle at the same time, P1; rep from * to last st, K1.

Rep rows 1–4 for patt.

Faggoted Rib

Multiple of 4 + 2

Row 1 (RS): K3, *YO, sl 1, K1, psso, K2; rep from * to last 3 sts, YO, sl 1, K1, psso, K1.

Row 2: P3, *YO, P2tog, P2; rep from * to last 3 sts, YO, P2tog, P1.

Rep rows 1 and 2 for patt.

Basket Weave Rib

Multiple of 15 + 8

Row 1 (RS): *P3, K2, P3, K1, (cross 2 front) 3 times; rep from * to last 8 sts, P3, K2, P3.

Row 2: *K3, cross 2 purl, K3, P1, (cross 2 purl) 3 times; rep from * to last 8 sts, K3, cross 2 purl, K3.

Rep rows 1 and 2 for patt.

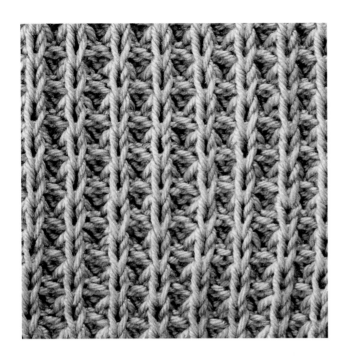

Chain-Stitch Rib

Multiple of 3 + 2

Row 1: K2, *P1, K2; rep from * to end.

Row 2 (RS): P2, *K1, P2; rep from * to end.

Row 3: Rep row 1.

Row 4: P2, *yb, insert needle through center of st 3 rows below next st on needle and knit this in the usual way, slipping st above it off needle at the same time; P2; rep from * to end.

Rep rows 1–4 for patt.

Linked Ribs

Multiple of 8 + 4

Row 1 (RS): P4, *K1, P2, K1, P4; rep from * to end.

Row 2: K4, *P1, K2, P1, K4; rep from * to end.

Rows 3 and 4: Rep rows 1 and 2.

Row 5: P4, *cross 2 left, cross 2 right, P4; rep from * to end.

Row 6: K4, *P4, K4; rep from * to end.

Rep rows 1–6 for patt.

Chevron Rib 1

Multiple of 18 + 1

Row 1 (RS): P1, *K1, P2, K2, P2, K1, P1; rep from * to end.

Row 2: *K3, P2, K2, P2, K1, (P2, K2) twice; rep from * to last st, K1.

Row 3: *(P2, K2) twice, P3, K2, P2, K2, P1; rep from * to last st, P1.

Row 4: *K1, P2, K2, P2, K5, P2, K2, P2; rep from * to last st, K1.

Rep rows 1–4 for patt.

Little Chevron Rib

Multiple of 10 + 1

Row 1 (RS): P1, *K1, P1, (K2, P1) twice, K1, P1; rep from * to end.

Row 2: K1, *P2, (K1, P1) twice, K1, P2, K1; rep from * to end.

Row 3: P1, *K3, P3, K3, P1; rep from * to end.

Row 4: K2, *P3, K1, P3, K3; rep from * to last 9 sts, P3, K1, P3, K2.

Rep rows 1–4 for patt.

Three-Stitch Twisted Rib

Multiple of 5 + 2

Row 1: K2, *P3, K2; rep from * to end.

Row 2 (RS): P2, *cross 3, P2; rep from * to end.

Rep rows 1 and 2 for patt.

Sailors' Rib

Multiple of 5 + 1

Row 1 (RS): K1 through back loop, *P1, K2, P1, K1 through back loop; rep from * to end.

Row 2: P1, *K1, P2, K1, P1; rep from * to end.

Row 3: K1 through back loop, *P4, K1 through back loop; rep from * to end.

Row 4: P1, *K4, P1; rep from * to end.

Rep rows 1–4 for patt.

Fancy Slip-Stitch Rib

Multiple of 5 + 2

Row 1 (RS): P2, *K1, sl 1, K1, P2; rep from * to end.

Row 2: K2, *P3, K2; rep from * to end.

Rep rows 1 and 2 for patt.

Supple Rib

Multiple of 3 + 1

Row 1 (RS): K1, *knit the next st but do not slip it off left-hand needle, then purl the same st and the next st tog, K1; rep from * to end.

Row 2: Purl.

Rep rows 1 and 2 for patt.

Uneven Rib

Multiple of 4 + 3

All rows: *K2, P2; rep from * to last 3 sts, K2, P1.

Rep row for patt.

Beaded Rib

Multiple of 5 + 2

Row 1 (RS): P2, *K1, P1, K1, P2; rep from * to end.

Row 2: K2, *P3, K2; rep from * to end.

Rep rows 1 and 2 for patt.

Farrow Rib

Multiple of 3 + 1

Row 1 (RS): *K2, P1; rep from * to last st, K1.

Row 2: P1, *K2, P1; rep from * to end.

Rep rows 1 and 2 for patt.

Puffed Rib

Multiple of 3 + 2

Row 1 (RS): P2, *YO, K1, YO, P2; rep from * to end.

Row 2: K2, *P3, K2; rep from * to end.

Row 3: P2, *K3, P2; rep from * to end.

Row 4: K2, *P3tog, K2; rep from * to end.

Rep rows 1–4 for patt.

Moss Rib

Multiple of 4 + 1

Row 1: K2, *P1, K3; rep from * to last 3 sts, P1, K2.

Row 2: P1, *K3, P1; rep from * to end.

Rep rows 1 and 2 for patt.

Corded Rib

Multiple of 4 + 2

All rows: K1, *K2tog through back loop, pick up horizontal strand of yarn lying between stitch just worked and next st and knit into back of it, P2; rep from * to last st, K1.

Rep row for patt.

Embossed Rib

Multiple of 6 + 2

Row 1 (RS): P2, *K1 through back loop, K1, P1, K1 through back loop, P2; rep from * to end.

Row 2: K2, *P1 through back loop, K1, P1, P1 through back loop, K2; rep from * to end.

Row 3: P2, *K1 through back loop, P1, K1, K1 through back loop, P2; rep from * to end.

Row 4: K2, *P1 through back loop, P1, K1, P1 through back loop, K2; rep from * to end.

Rep these 4 rows.

Knotted Rib

Multiple of 5

Row 1 (RS): P2, *knit into front and back of next st, P4; rep from * to last 3 sts, knit into front and back of next st, P2.

Row 2: K2, *P2tog, K4; rep from * to last 4 sts, P2tog, K2.

Rep rows 1 and 2 for patt.

Piqué Rib

Multiple of 10 + 3

Row 1 (RS): K3, *P3, K1, P3, K3; rep from *
to end.

Row 2: P3, *K3, P1, K3, P3; rep from * to end.

Row 3: Rep row 1.

Row 4: Knit.

Rep rows 1–4 for patt.

Bobble Rib

Multiple of 8 + 3

Row 1 (RS): K3, *P2, (P1, K1) twice into next st,
pass the first 3 of these sts, one at a time,
over the fourth st (bobble made), P2, K3;
rep from * to end.

Row 2: P3, *K2, P1, K2, P3; rep from * to end.

Row 3: K3, *P2, K1, P2, K3; rep from * to end.

Row 4: Rep row 2.

Rep rows 1–4 for patt.

Shadow Rib

Multiple of 3 + 2

Row 1 (RS): Knit.

Row 2: P2, *K1 through back loop, P2; rep from * to end.

Rep rows 1 and 2 for patt.

Blanket Rib

Multiple of 2 + 1

Row 1 (RS): Knit into front and back of each st (thus doubling the number of sts).

Row 2: K2tog, *P2tog, K2tog; rep from * to end (original number of sts restored).

Rep rows 1 and 2 for patt.

Seeded Rib

Multiple of 4 + 1

Row 1 (RS): P1, *K3, P1; rep from * to end.

Row 2: K2, P1, *K3, P1; rep from * to last 2 sts, K2.

Rep rows 1 and 2 for patt.

Two-Stitch Rib

Multiple of 4 + 2

All rows: K2, *P2, K2; rep from * to end.

Rep row for patt.

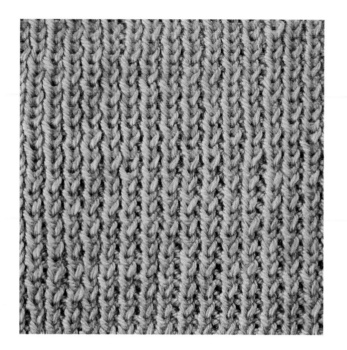

Knit-One, Purl-One Rib

Multiple of 2

All rows: *K1, P1; rep from * to end.

Rep row for patt.

Knit-Two, Purl-Two Rib

Multiple of 4

All rows: *K2, P2; rep from * to end.

Rep row for patt.

Brioche Rib

Multiple of 2

Row 1: Knit.

Row 2 (RS): *K1, K1 in st below; rep from * to last 2 sts, K2.

Rep row 2 for patt.

Polperro Northcott

Multiple of 4 + 2

Row 1–3: Knit.

Row 4 (WS): K2, *P2, K2; rep from * to end.

Row 5: Knit.

Rows 6–25: Rep rows 4 and 5 ten more times.

Rows 26 and 27: Knit.

Row 28: Purl.

Rep rows 1–28 for patt.

Double Lace Rib

Multiple of 6 + 2

Row 1 (RS): K2, *P1, YO, K2tog through back loop, P1, K2; rep from * to end.

Row 2: P2, *K1, P2; rep from * to end.

Row 3: K2, *P1, K2tog, YO, P1, K2; rep from * to end.

Row 4: Rep row 2.

Rep rows 1–4 for patt.

Woven Rib

Multiple of 6 + 3

Row 1 (RS): P3, *sl 1 wyif, K1, sl 1 wyif, P3; rep from * to end.

Row 2: K3, *P3, K3; rep from * to end.

Row 3: *P3, K1, sl 1 wyif, K1; rep from * to last 3 sts, P3.

Row 4: Rep row 2.

Rep rows 1–4 for patt.

Cluster Rib

Multiple of 3 + 1

Row 1 (RS): P1, *K2, P1; rep from * to end.

Row 2: K1, *YO, K2, slip YO over the 2 knit sts, K1; rep from * to end.

Rep rows 1 and 2 for patt.

Harris-Tweed Rib

Multiple of 4 + 2

Row 1 (RS): K2, *P2, K2; rep from * to end.

Row 2: P2, *K2, P2; rep from * to end.

Row 3: Knit.

Row 4: Purl.

Rows 5 and 6: Rep rows 1 and 2.

Row 7: Purl.

Row 8: Knit.

Rep rows 1–8 for patt.

Hunter's Stitch

Multiple of 11 + 4

Row 1 (RS): P4, *(K1 through back loop, P1) 3 times, K1 through back loop, P4; rep from * to end.

Row 2: K4, *P1 (K1 through back loop, P1) 3 times, K4; rep from * to end.

Rep rows 1 and 2 for patt.

Speckle Rib

Multiple of 2 + 1

Row 1 (RS): Knit.

Row 2: Purl.

Row 3: K1, *sl 1, K1; rep from * to end.

Row 4: K1, *sl 1 wyif, K1; rep from * to end.

Row 5: Knit.

Row 6: Purl.

Row 7: K2, *sl 1, K1; rep from * to last st, K1.

Row 8: K2, *sl 1 wyif, K1; rep from * to last st, K1.

Rep rows 1–8 for patt.

Medallion Rib

Multiple of 8 + 4

Row 1 (RS): P4, *sl 2 wyib, cross 2 back, P4;
rep from * to end.

Row 2: K4, *sl 2 wyif, purl second st on left-
hand needle, then first st, slipping both sts
from needle tog, K4; rep from * to end.

Row 3: Knit.

Row 4: Purl.

Rep rows 1–4 for patt.

Waving Rib Pattern

Multiple of 6 + 2

Row 1 (RS): P2, *K4, P2; rep from * to end.

Row 2: K2, *P4, K2; rep from * to end.

Rows 3 and 4: Rep rows 1 and 2.

Row 5: K3, P2, *K4, P2; rep from * to last
3 sts, K3.

Row 6: P3, K2, *P4, K2; rep from * to last
3 sts, P3.

Rows 7 and 8: Rep rows 5 and 6.

Rep rows 1–8 for patt.

Mini Bobble Stitch

Multiple of 2 + 1

Row 1 (RS): Knit.

Row 2: K1, *MB, K1; rep from * to end.

Row 3: Knit.

Row 4: K2, *MB, K1; rep from * to last st, K1.

Rep rows 1–4 for patt.

Lacy Bubbles

Multiple of 6 + 3

Row 1 (RS): Purl.

Row 2: Knit.

Row 3: Purl.

Row 4: K1, P3tog, (K1, P1, K1, P1, K1) into next st, *P5tog, (K1, P1, K1, P1, K1) into next st; rep from * to last 4 sts, P3tog, K1.

Row 5: Purl.

Row 6: K1, (K1, P1, K1) into next st, P5tog, *(K1, P1, K1, P1, K1) into next st, P5tog; rep from * to last 2 sts, (K1, P1, K1) into next st, K1.

Row 7: Purl.

Row 8: Knit.

Rep rows 1–8 for patt.

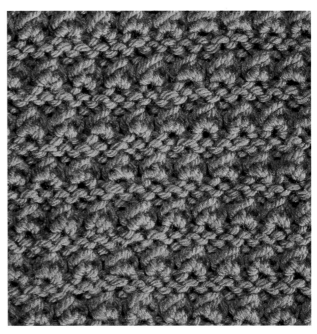

Trinity Stitch

Multiple of 4 + 2

Row 1 (WS): K1, *(K1, P1, K1) into next st, P3tog; rep from * to last st, K1.

Row 2: Purl.

Row 3: K1, *P3tog, (K1, P1, K1) into next st; rep from * to last st, K1.

Row 4: Purl.

Rep rows 1–4 for patt.

Horizontal Ridge Stitch

Multiple of 2

Row 1: Purl.

Row 2: *K1, (K1, P1, K1) into next st; rep from * to end.

Row 3: *K3, P1; rep from * to end.

Row 4: *K1, P3tog; rep from * to end.

Row 5: Purl.

Row 6: *(K1, P1, K1) into next st, K1; rep from * to end.

Row 7: *P1, K3; rep from * to end.

Row 8: *P3tog, K1; rep from * to end.

Rep rows 1–8 for patt.

Alternating Bobble Stitch

Multiple of 6 + 2

Row 1 and all odd rows (RS): Knit.

Row 2: Purl.

Row 4: P1, *P4, make bobble: P2 (turn, sl 1 wyib, K1, turn, sl 1 wyif, P1) 3 times; rep from * to last st, P1.

Row 6: Purl.

Row 8: P1, *make bobble as before, P4; rep from * to last st, P1.

Rep rows 1–8 for patt.

Bramble Stitch

Multiple of 4 + 2

Row 1 (RS): Purl.

Row 2: K1, *(K1, P1, K1) into next st, P3tog; rep from * to last st, K1.

Row 3: Purl.

Row 4: K1, *P3tog, (K1, P1, K1) into next st; rep from * to last st, K1.

Rep rows 1–4 for patt.

Berry Stitch

Multiple of 4 + 3

Row 1 (RS): K1, (K1, K1 through back loop, K1) into next st, *P3, (K1, K1 through back loop, K1) into next st; rep from * to last st, K1.

Row 2: K4, P3tog, *K3, P3tog; rep from * to last 4 sts, K4.

Row 3: K1, P3, *(K1, K1 through back loop, K1) into next st, P3; rep from * to last st, K1.

Row 4: K1, P3tog, *K3, P3tog; rep from * to last st, K1.

Rep rows 1–4 for patt.

Knot Pattern

Multiple of 6 + 5

Row 1 (RS): Knit.

Row 2: Purl.

Row 3: K1, *MK, K3; rep from * to last 4 sts, MK, K1.

Row 4: Purl.

Row 5: Knit.

Row 6: Purl.

Row 7: K4, *MK, K3; rep from * to last st, K1.

Row 8: Purl.

Rep rows 1–8 for patt.

Diagonal Knot Stitch

Multiple of 3 + 1

Row 1 and all odd rows (RS): Knit.

Row 2: *MK; rep from * to last st, P1.

Row 4: P2, *MK; rep from * to last 2 sts, P2.

Row 6: P1, *MK; rep from * to end.

Rep rows 1–6 for patt.

Spaced Knots

Multiple of 6 + 5

Rows 1–4: Work in St st, starting with a knit row.

Row 5 (RS): K5, *(K1, P1) twice into next st, K5; rep from * to end.

Row 6: P5, *sl 3, K1, pass 3 sl sts separately over last st (knot completed), P5; rep from * to end.

Rows 7–10: Work in St st, starting with a knit row.

Row 11: K2, *(K1, P1) twice into next st, K5; rep from * to last 3 sts, (K1, P1) twice into next st, K2.

Row 12: P2, *sl 3, K1, pass sl sts over as before, P5; rep from * to last 6 sts, sl 3, K1, pass sl sts over as before, P2.

Rep rows 1–12 for patt.

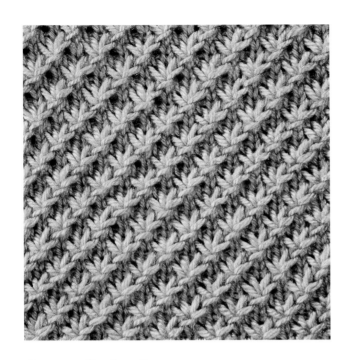

Star Stitch

Multiple of 4 + 1

Row 1 (RS): Knit.

Row 2: P1, *MS, P1; rep from * to end.

Row 3: Knit.

Row 4: P3, MS, *P1, MS; rep from * to last 3 sts, P3.

Rep rows 1–4 for patt.

Garter and Slip Stitch

Multiple of 6 + 4

Row 1 (RS): Knit.

Row 2: K1, *sl 2 wyif, K4; rep from * to last 3 sts, sl 2 wyif, K1.

Row 3: K1, *sl 2 wyib, K4; rep from * to last 3 sts, sl 2, K1.

Rows 4 and 5: Rep rows 2 and 3.

Row 6: Rep row 2.

Row 7: Knit.

Row 8: K4, *sl 2 wyif, K4; rep from * to end.

Row 9: K4, *sl 2 wyib, K4; rep from * to end.

Rows 10 and 11: Rep rows 8 and 9.

Row 12: Rep row 8.

Rep rows 1–12 for patt.

Slip-Stitch Stripes

Multiple of 5

Row 1 (WS): K2, *P1, K4; rep from * to last 3 sts, P1, K2.

Row 2: K2, *sl 1, K4; rep from * to last 3 sts, sl 1, K2.

Rep rows 1 and 2 for patt.

Garter Slip Stitch 1

Multiple of 2 + 1

Rows 1 and 2: Knit.

Row 3 (RS): K1, *sl 1, K1; rep from * to end.

Row 4: K1, *sl 1 wyif, K1; rep from * to end.

Rep rows 1–4 for patt.

Garter Slip Stitch 2

Multiple of 2 + 1

Row 1 (RS): Knit.

Row 2: Knit.

Row 3: K1, *sl 1, K1; rep from * to end.

Row 4: K1, *sl 1 wyif, K1; rep from * to end.

Rows 5 and 6: Knit.

Row 7: K2, *sl 1, K1; rep from * to last st, K1.

Row 8: K2, *sl 1 wyif, K1; rep from * to last st, K1.

Rep rows 1–8 for patt.

Garter Slip Stitch 3

Multiple of 2 + 1

Row 1 (WS): Knit.

Row 2: Knit.

Row 3: K1, *sl 1, K1; rep from * to end.

Row 4: Knit.

Rep rows 1–4 for patt.

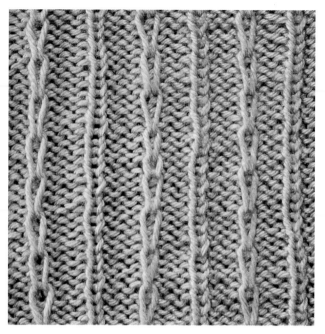

Ridged Slip Stitch

Multiple of 4 + 2

Row 1 (RS): K1, *K3, sl 1 wyib; rep from * to last st, K1.

Row 2: P1, *sl 1 wyif, P3; rep from * to last st, P1.

Row 3: Rep row 1.

Row 4: Knit.

Row 5: K1, *K1, sl 1 wyib, K2; rep from * to last st, K1.

Row 6: P1, *P2, sl 1 wyif, P1; rep from * to last st, P1.

Row 7: Rep row 5.

Row 8: Knit.

Rep rows 1–8 for patt.

Slip-Stitch Ribbing

Multiple of 8 + 3

Row 1 (RS): P3, *K1 (wrapping yarn twice around needle), P3, K1, P3; rep from * to end.

Row 2: K3, *P1, K3, sl 1 wyif (dropping extra loop), K3; rep from * to end.

Row 3: P3, *sl 1 wyib, P3, K1, P3; rep from * to end.

Row 4: K3, *P1, K3, sl 1 wyif, K3; rep from * to end.

Rep rows 1–4 for patt.

Slipped Rib 1

Multiple of 2 + 1

Row 1 (RS): K1, *sl 1 wyif, K1; rep from * to end.

Row 2: Purl.

Rep rows 1 and 2 for patt.

Slipped Rib 2

Multiple of 4 + 3

Row 1 (RS): K1, sl 1, *K3, sl 1; rep from * to last st, K1.

Row 2: P1, sl 1, *P3, sl 1; rep from * to last st, P1.

Row 3: *K3, sl 1; rep from * to last 3 sts, K3.

Row 4: *P3, sl 1; rep from * to last 3 sts, P3.

Rep rows 1–4 for patt.

Medallion Stitch

Multiple of 4 + 2

Row 1 (RS): K1, *sl 2 wyib, K into back of second st on left-hand needle; then K first st, slipping both sts from needle tog; rep from * to last st, K1.

Row 2: K1, *sl 2 wyif, P second st on left-hand needle; then P first st, slipping both sts from needle tog; rep from * to last st, K1.

Row 3: Knit.

Row 4: Purl.

Rep rows 1–4 for patt.

Mock Rib

Multiple of 2 + 1

Row 1 (RS): K1, *P1, K1; rep from * to end.

Row 2: P1, *sl 1 wyif, P1; rep from * to end.

Rep rows 1 and 2 for patt.

Double Mock Rib

Multiple of 4 + 2

Row 1 (RS): K2, *P2, K2; rep from * to end.

Row 2: P2, *sl 2 wyif, P2; rep from * to end.

Rep rows 1 and 2 for patt.

Houndstooth Pattern

Multiple of 3

Cast on in color A.

Row 1 (RS): Using color A, K1, *sl 1, K2; rep from * to last 2 sts, sl 1, K1.

Row 2: Using color A, purl.

Row 3: Using color B, *sl 1, K2; rep from * to end.

Row 4: Using color B, purl.

Rep rows 1–4 for patt.

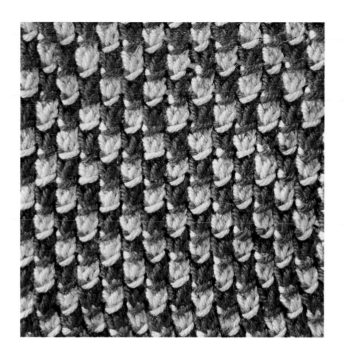

Two-Color Elm-Seed Pattern

Multiple of 4 + 2

Row 1 (RS): K1, *K2 with color A, K2 with color B; rep from * to last st, K1.

Row 2: K1, *YO with color A, P2, pass YO over last 2 sts; rep from * with color B; rep from first *, alternating colors, to last st, K1.

Row 3: K1, *K2 with color B, K2 with color A; rep from * to last st, K1.

Row 4: K1, *YO with color B, P2, pass YO over last 2 sts; rep from * with color A; rep from first *, alternating colors, to last st; K1.

Rep rows 1–4 for patt.

Bicolor Tweed Stitch

Multiple of 4 + 3

Foundation row: With color A, purl.

Row 1 (RS): With color B, K1, *sl 1 wyif, K3; rep from * to last 2 sts, sl 1 wyif, K1.

Row 2: With color B, K1, sl 1 wyif, *P3, sl 1 wyif; rep from * to last st, K1.

Row 3: With color A, K1, *K2, sl 1 wyif, K1; rep from * to last 2 sts, K2.

Row 4: With color A, K1, P2, *sl 1 wyif, P3; rep from * to last 4 sts, sl 1 wyif, P2, K1.

Rep rows 1–4 for patt.

Twisted Knit Tweed

Multiple of 2 + 1

Foundation rows: Using color A, knit 2 rows.

Row 1 (RS): Using color B, K1, *K1 in st below, K1; rep from * to end.

Row 2: Using color B, knit.

Row 3: Using color A, K1 in row below, *K1, K1 in st below; rep from * to end.

Row 4: Using color A, knit.

Rep rows 1–4 for patt.

Houndstooth Tweed

Multiple of 3

Cast on in color A.

Row 1 (RS): Using color A, *K2, sl 1; rep from * to end.

Row 2: Using color A, knit.

Row 3: Using color B, *sl 1, K2; rep from * to end.

Row 4: Using color B, knit.

Rep rows 1–4 for patt.

Abbreviations

K	knit	**P4tog**	purl 4 stitches together
K2tog	knit 2 stitches together	**rep**	repeat
K3tog	knit 3 stitches together	**RS**	right side
M1	make 1 (see "Special Instructions")	**sl**	slip stitch purlwise unless otherwise instructed
MB	make bobble (see "Special Instructions")	**st(s)**	stitch(es)
MK	make knot (see "Special Instructions")	**St st**	stockinette stitch (knit 1 row; purl 1 row)
MS	make star (see "Special Instructions")	**tog**	together
P	purl	**WS**	wrong side
psso	pass slipped stitch over	**wyib**	with yarn in back
p2sso	pass 2 slipped stitches over	**wyif**	with yarn in front
P2tog	purl 2 stitches together	**yb**	yarn back
P3tog	purl 3 stitches together	**yf**	yarn forward
		YO	yarn over

Special Instructions

Cable 3 left:
Slip the next stitch onto a cable needle and hold at the front of your work, knit the next 2 stitches from the left-hand needle; then knit the stitch from the cable needle.

Cable 3 right:
Slip the next 2 stitches onto a cable needle and hold at the back of your work, knit the next stitch from the left-hand needle; then knit the 2 stitches from the cable needle.

Cable 4 back or cable 4 front:
Slip the next 2 stitches onto a cable needle and hold at the back (or front) of your work, knit the next 2 stitches from the left-hand needle; then knit the 2 stitches from the cable needle.

Cable 6 back or cable 6 front:
Slip the next 3 stitches onto a cable needle and hold at the back (or front) of your work, knit the next 3 stitches from the left-hand needle; then knit the 3 stitches from the cable needle.

Cable 8 back or cable 8 front:
Slip the next 4 stitches onto a cable needle and hold at the back (or front) of your work, knit the next 4 stitches from the left-hand needle; then knit the 4 stitches from the cable needle.

Cable 10 back or cable 10 front:
Slip the next 5 stitches onto a cable needle and hold at the back (or front) of your work, knit the next 5 stitches from the left-hand needle; then knit the 5 stitches from the cable needle.

Cable 12 back or cable 12 front:
Slip the next 6 stitches onto a cable needle and hold at the back (or front) of your work, knit the next 6 stitches from the left-hand needle; then knit the 6 stitches from the cable needle.

Cross 2 back or cross 2 front:
Knit into the back (or front) of the 2nd stitch on the needle; then knit the first stitch, slipping both stitches off the needle at the same time.

Cross 2 left:
Slip the next stitch onto a cable needle and hold at the front of your work, knit the next stitch from the left-hand needle; then knit the stitch from the cable needle.

Cross 2 right:
Slip the next stitch onto a cable needle and hold at the back of your work, knit the next stitch from the left-hand needle; then knit the stitch from the cable needle.

Cross 2 purl:
Purl into the front of the second stitch on the needle; then purl the first stitch, slipping both stitches off the needle together.

Cross 3:
Knit into the front of the third stitch on the needle; then knit the first stitch in the usual way, slipping this stitch off the needle. Now knit the second stitch in the usual way, slipping the second and third stitches off the needle together.

Cross 3 back:
Slip the next stitch onto a cable needle and hold at the back of your work, knit the next 2 stitches from the left-hand needle; then knit the stitch from the cable needle.

Cross 3 front:
Slip the next 2 stitches onto a cable needle and hold at the front of your work, knit the next stitch from the left-hand needle; then knit the 2 stitches from the cable needle.

Cross 3 together:
Slip the next 2 stitches onto a cable needle and hold at the back of your work, knit the next stitch from the left-hand needle; then knit together the 2 stitches from the cable needle.

Cross 4 back:
Knit into the back of the fourth stitch on the needle; then knit the first stitch in the usual way, slipping this stitch off the needle. Now knit the second and third stitches in the usual way, slipping the third and fourth stitches off the needle together.

Cross 4 front:
Knit into the front of the fourth stitch on the needle; then knit the first stitch in the usual way, slipping this stitch off the needle. Now knit the second and third stitches in the usual way, slipping the third and fourth stitches off the needle together.

Cross 4 left:
Slip the next stitch onto a cable needle and hold at the front of your work, knit the next 3 stitches from the left-hand needle; then knit the stitch from the cable needle.

Cross 4 right:
Slip the next 3 stitches onto a cable needle and hold at the back of your work, knit the next stitch from the left-hand needle; then knit the 3 stitches from the cable needle.

Cross 6:

Slip the next 4 stitches onto a cable needle and hold at the front of your work, knit the next 2 stitches from the left-hand needle; then slip 2 stitches from the cable needle back to the left-hand needle. Pass the cable needle with the 2 remaining stitches to the back of your work, purl the 2 stitches from the left-hand needle; then knit the 2 stitches from the cable needle.

K1 in st below:

Insert the needle into the center of the stitch below the next stitch on the needle and knit in the usual way, slipping the stitch above it off the needle at the same time.

Make 1:

Insert the left-hand needle from the back to the front into the horizontal strand of yarn lying between the stitch just worked and the next stitch. Knit through the front loop.

Make bobble:

(Purl 1, knit 1, purl 1, knit 1) all into the next stitch; pass the second, third, and fourth stitches over the first stitch.

Make knot:

Purl 3 stitches together, leaving the stitches on the left-hand needle. Wrap the yarn around the needle; then purl the same 3 stitches together again.

Make star:

See "Make knot."

Twist 2 left:

Slip the next stitch onto a cable needle and hold at the front of your work, purl the next stitch from the left-hand needle; then knit through the back loop of the stitch on the cable needle.

Twist 2 right:

Slip the next stitch onto a cable needle and hold at the back of your work, knit through the back loop of the next stitch on the left-hand needle; then purl the stitch from the cable needle.

Twist 3 back:

Slip the next stitch onto a cable needle and hold at the back of your work, knit the next 2 stitches from the left-hand needle; then purl the stitch from the cable needle.

Twist 3 front:

Slip the next 2 stitches onto a cable needle and hold at the front of your work, purl the next stitch from the left-hand needle; then knit the 2 stitches from the cable needle.

Twist 4 back:

Slip the next 2 stitches onto a cable needle and hold at the back of your work, knit the next 2 stitches from the left-hand needle; then purl the 2 stitches from the cable needle.

Twist 4 front:

Slip the next 2 stitches onto a cable needle and hold at the front of your work, purl the next 2 stitches from the left-hand needle; then knit the 2 stitches from the cable needle.

Twist 6 back:

Slip the next 3 stitches onto a cable needle and hold at the back of your work, knit the next 3 stitches from the left-hand needle; then purl the 3 stitches from the cable needle.

Twist 6 front:

Slip the next 3 stitches onto a cable needle and hold at the front of your work, purl the next 3 stitches from the left-hand needle; then knit the 3 stitches from the cable needle.

Stitch Index